"After utilizing toolkits from The Art of Service, I was able to identify threats within my organization to which I was completely unaware. Using my team's knowledge as a competitive advantage, we now have superior systems that save time and energy."

"As a new Chief Technology Officer, I was feeling unprepared and inadequate to be successful in my role. I ordered an IT toolkit Sunday night and was prepared Monday morning to shed light on areas of improvement within my organization. I no longer felt overwhelmed and intimidated, I was excited to share what I had learned."

"I used the questionnaires to interview members of my team. I never knew how many insights we could produce collectively with our internal knowledge."

"I usually work until at least 8pm on weeknights. The Art of Service questionnaire saved me so much time and worry that Thursday night I attended my son's soccer game without sacrificing my professional obligations."

"After purchasing The Art of Service toolkit, I was able to identify areas where my company was not in compliance that could have put my job at risk. I looked like a hero when I proactively educated my team on the risks and presented a solid solution."

"I spent months shopping for an external consultant before realizing that The Art of Service would allow my team to consult themselves! Not only did we save time not catching a consultant up to speed, we were able to keep our company information and industry secrets confidential."

"Everyday there are new regulations and processes in my industry. The Art of Service toolkit has kept me ahead by using AI technology to constantly update the toolkits and address emerging needs."

"I customized The Art of Service toolkit to focus specifically on the concerns of my role and industry. I didn't have to waste time with a generic self-help book that wasn't tailored to my exact situation."

"Many of our competitors have asked us about our secret sauce. When I tell them it's the knowledge we have in-house, they never believe me. Little do they know The Art of Service toolkits are working behind the scenes."

"One of my friends hired a consultant who used the knowledge gained working with his company to advise their competitor. Talk about a competitive disadvantage! The Art of Service allowed us to keep our knowledge from walking out the door along with a huge portion of our budget in consulting fees."

"Honestly, I didn't know what I didn't know. Before purchasing The Art of Service, I didn't realize how many areas of my business needed to be refreshed and improved. I am so relieved The Art of Service was there to highlight our blind spots."

"Before The Art of Service, I waited eagerly for consulting company reports to come out each month. These reports kept us up to speed but provided little value because they put our competitors on the same playing field. With The Art of Service, we have uncovered unique insights to drive our business forward."

"Instead of investing extensive resources into an external consultant, we can spend more of our budget towards pursuing our company goals and objectives…while also spending a little more on corporate holiday parties."

"The risk of our competitors getting ahead has been mitigated because The Art of Service has provided us with a 360-degree view of threats within our organization before they even arise."

D2L
Complete Self-Assessment Guide

Notice of rights

You are licensed to use the Self-Assessment contents in your presentations and materials for internal use and customers without asking us - we are here to help.

Trademarks

Table of Contents

About The Art of Service

The Art of Service, Business Process Architects since 2000, is dedicated to helping stakeholders achieve excellence.

Defining, designing, creating, and implementing a process to solve a stakeholders challenge or meet an objective is the most valuable role… In EVERY group, company, organization and department.

Unless you're talking a one-time, single-use project, there should be a process. Whether that process is managed and implemented by humans, AI, or a combination of the two, it needs to be designed by someone with a complex enough perspective to ask the right questions.

Someone capable of asking the right questions and step back and say, 'What are we really trying to accomplish here? And is there a different way to look at it?'

With The Art of Service's Self-Assessments, we empower people who can do just that — whether their title is marketer, entrepreneur, manager, salesperson, consultant, Business Process Manager, executive assistant, IT Manager, CIO etc... —they are the people who rule the future. They are people who watch the process as it happens, and ask the right questions to make the process work better.

Contact us when you need any support with this Self-Assessment and any help with templates, blue-prints and examples of standard documents you might need:

https://theartofservice.com
support@theartofservice.com

Included Resources - how to access

Included with your purchase of the book is the D2L Self-

Assessment Spreadsheet Dashboard which contains all questions and Self-Assessment areas and auto-generates insights, graphs, and project RACI planning - all with examples to get you started right away.

How? Simply send an email to
access@theartofservice.com
with this books' title in the subject to get the D2L Self Assessment Tool right away.

The auto reply will guide you further, you will then receive the following contents with New and Updated specific criteria:

- The latest quick edition of the book in PDF

- The latest complete edition of the book in PDF, which criteria correspond to the criteria in...

- The Self-Assessment Excel Dashboard, and...

- Example pre-filled Self-Assessment Excel Dashboard to get familiar with results generation

- In-depth specific Checklists covering the topic

- Project management checklists and templates to assist with implementation

INCLUDES LIFETIME SELF ASSESSMENT UPDATES

Every self assessment comes with Lifetime Updates and Lifetime Free Updated Books. Lifetime Updates is an industry-first feature which allows you to receive verified self assessment updates, ensuring you always have the most accurate information at your fingertips.

Get it now- you will be glad you did - do it now, before you forget.

Send an email to **access@theartofservice.com** with this books' title in the subject to get the D2L Self Assessment Tool right away.

Purpose of this Self-Assessment

This Self-Assessment has been developed to improve understanding of the requirements and elements of D2L, based on best practices and standards in business process architecture, design and quality management.

It is designed to allow for a rapid Self-Assessment to determine how closely existing management practices and procedures correspond to the elements of the Self-Assessment.

The criteria of requirements and elements of D2L have been rephrased in the format of a Self-Assessment questionnaire, with a seven-criterion scoring system, as explained in this document.

In this format, even with limited background knowledge of D2L, a manager can quickly review existing operations to determine how they measure up to the standards. This in turn can serve as the starting point of a 'gap analysis' to identify management tools or system elements that might usefully be implemented in the organization to help improve overall performance.

How to use the Self-Assessment

On the following pages are a series of questions to identify to what extent your D2L initiative is complete in comparison to the requirements set in standards.

To facilitate answering the questions, there is a space in front of each question to enter a score on a scale of '1' to '5'.

1 Strongly Disagree

2 Disagree

3 Neutral

4 Agree

5 Strongly Agree

Read the question and rate it with the following in front of mind:

'In my belief,
the answer to this question is clearly defined'.

There are two ways in which you can choose to interpret this statement;
1. how aware are you that the answer to the question is clearly defined
2. for more in-depth analysis you can choose to gather evidence and confirm the answer to the question. This obviously will take more time, most Self-Assessment users opt for the first way to interpret the question and dig deeper later on based on the outcome of the overall Self-Assessment.

A score of '1' would mean that the answer is not clear at all, where a '5' would mean the answer is crystal clear and defined. Leave emtpy when the question is not applicable or you don't want to answer it, you can skip it without affecting your score. Write your score in the space provided.

After you have responded to all the appropriate statements in each section, compute your average score for that section, using the formula provided, and round to the nearest tenth. Then transfer to the corresponding spoke in the D2L Scorecard on the second next page of the Self-Assessment.

Your completed D2L Scorecard will give you a clear presentation of which D2L areas need attention.

D2L
Scorecard Example

Example of how the finalized Scorecard can look like:

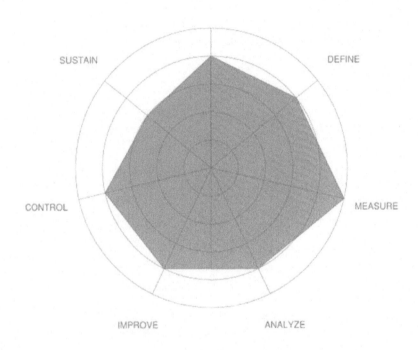

D2L
Scorecard

Your Scores:

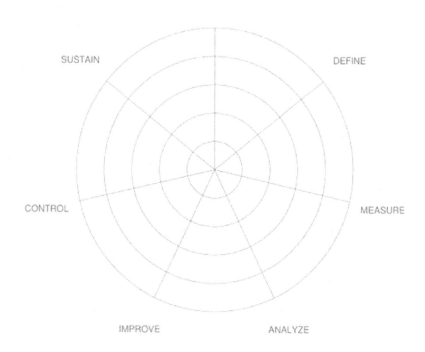

BEGINNING OF THE SELF-ASSESSMENT:

CRITERION #1: RECOGNIZE

INTENT: Be aware of the need for change. Recognize that there is an unfavorable variation, problem or symptom.

In my belief, the answer to this question is clearly defined:

5 Strongly Agree

4 Agree

3 Neutral

2 Disagree

1 Strongly Disagree

1. Can management personnel recognize the monetary benefit of D2L?
<--- Score

2. Are you dealing with any of the same issues today as yesterday? What can you do about this?
<--- Score

3. Do you recognize D2L achievements?

<--- Score

4. What D2L capabilities do you need?
<--- Score

5. Does the problem have ethical dimensions?
<--- Score

6. To what extent would your organization benefit from being recognized as a award recipient?
<--- Score

7. Will new equipment/products be required to facilitate D2L delivery, for example is new software needed?
<--- Score

8. What are the stakeholder objectives to be achieved with D2L?
<--- Score

9. Consider your own D2L project, what types of organizational problems do you think might be causing or affecting your problem, based on the work done so far?
<--- Score

10. What is the D2L problem definition? What do you need to resolve?
<--- Score

11. How are the D2L's objectives aligned to the group's overall stakeholder strategy?
<--- Score

12. What else needs to be measured?

<--- Score

13. What information do users need?
<--- Score

14. What is the smallest subset of the problem you can usefully solve?
<--- Score

15. What are the timeframes required to resolve each of the issues/problems?
<--- Score

16. Who should resolve the D2L issues?
<--- Score

17. Will it solve real problems?
<--- Score

18. What vendors make products that address the D2L needs?
<--- Score

19. How many trainings, in total, are needed?
<--- Score

20. Is the quality assurance team identified?
<--- Score

21. What is the problem and/or vulnerability?
<--- Score

22. Where is training needed?
<--- Score

23. Think about the people you identified for your D2L

project and the project responsibilities you would assign to them, what kind of training do you think they would need to perform these responsibilities effectively?
<--- Score

24. How do you assess your D2L workforce capability and capacity needs, including skills, competencies, and staffing levels?
<--- Score

25. For your D2L project, identify and describe the business environment, is there more than one layer to the business environment?
<--- Score

26. How much are sponsors, customers, partners, stakeholders involved in D2L? In other words, what are the risks, if D2L does not deliver successfully?
<--- Score

27. Does your organization need more D2L education?
<--- Score

28. What are the minority interests and what amount of minority interests can be recognized?
<--- Score

29. Would you recognize a threat from the inside?
<--- Score

30. What are your needs in relation to D2L skills, labor, equipment, and markets?
<--- Score

31. What should be considered when identifying available resources, constraints, and deadlines?
<--- Score

32. How are you going to measure success?
<--- Score

33. What would happen if D2L weren't done?
<--- Score

34. Are controls defined to recognize and contain problems?
<--- Score

35. When a D2L manager recognizes a problem, what options are available?
<--- Score

36. Which information does the D2L business case need to include?
<--- Score

37. How do you identify subcontractor relationships?
<--- Score

38. What are the clients issues and concerns?
<--- Score

39. Is it clear when you think of the day ahead of you what activities and tasks you need to complete?
<--- Score

40. What extra resources will you need?
<--- Score

41. Are there any specific expectations or concerns

about the D2L team, D2L itself?
<--- Score

42. Are there any revenue recognition issues?
<--- Score

43. Did you miss any major D2L issues?
<--- Score

44. What is the recognized need?
<--- Score

45. What needs to be done?
<--- Score

46. What does D2L success mean to the stakeholders?
<--- Score

47. How do you recognize an objection?
<--- Score

48. Is the need for organizational change recognized?
<--- Score

49. What is the problem or issue?
<--- Score

50. How do you recognize an D2L objection?
<--- Score

51. How does it fit into your organizational needs and tasks?
<--- Score

52. Who else hopes to benefit from it?
<--- Score

53. What situation(s) led to this D2L Self Assessment?
<--- Score

54. Which needs are not included or involved?
<--- Score

55. Are there D2L problems defined?
<--- Score

56. Who needs to know about D2L?
<--- Score

57. Are employees recognized or rewarded for performance that demonstrates the highest levels of integrity?
<--- Score

58. What D2L coordination do you need?
<--- Score

59. Who needs what information?
<--- Score

60. What activities does the governance board need to consider?
<--- Score

61. What needs to stay?
<--- Score

62. What D2L problem should be solved?
<--- Score

63. What tools and technologies are needed for a custom D2L project?

<--- Score

64. Do you need different information or graphics?
<--- Score

65. Does D2L create potential expectations in other areas that need to be recognized and considered?
<--- Score

66. Where do you need to exercise leadership?
<--- Score

67. Who needs to know?
<--- Score

68. What training and capacity building actions are needed to implement proposed reforms?
<--- Score

69. How can auditing be a preventative security measure?
<--- Score

70. Have you identified your D2L key performance indicators?
<--- Score

71. What prevents you from making the changes you know will make you a more effective D2L leader?
<--- Score

72. What do employees need in the short term?
<--- Score

73. Do you know what you need to know about D2L?
<--- Score

74. How are training requirements identified?
<--- Score

75. As a sponsor, customer or management, how important is it to meet goals, objectives?
<--- Score

76. Looking at each person individually – does every one have the qualities which are needed to work in this group?
<--- Score

77. To what extent does each concerned units management team recognize D2L as an effective investment?
<--- Score

78. Whom do you really need or want to serve?
<--- Score

79. Will D2L deliverables need to be tested and, if so, by whom?
<--- Score

80. Will a response program recognize when a crisis occurs and provide some level of response?
<--- Score

81. Are problem definition and motivation clearly presented?
<--- Score

82. Who defines the rules in relation to any given issue?
<--- Score

83. What D2L events should you attend?
<--- Score

84. Are losses recognized in a timely manner?
<--- Score

85. What problems are you facing and how do you consider D2L will circumvent those obstacles?
<--- Score

86. Who are your key stakeholders who need to sign off?
<--- Score

87. Do you need to avoid or amend any D2L activities?
<--- Score

88. What do you need to start doing?
<--- Score

89. What are the D2L resources needed?
<--- Score

90. How do you identify the kinds of information that you will need?
<--- Score

91. Are your goals realistic? Do you need to redefine your problem? Perhaps the problem has changed or maybe you have reached your goal and need to set a new one?
<--- Score

92. What are the expected benefits of D2L to the stakeholder?

<--- Score

93. What creative shifts do you need to take?
<--- Score

94. What is the extent or complexity of the D2L problem?
<--- Score

95. Who needs budgets?
<--- Score

96. Is it needed?
<--- Score

Add up total points for this section:
_____ = Total points for this section

Divided by: _____ (number of statements answered) = _____
Average score for this section

Transfer your score to the D2L Index at the beginning of the Self-Assessment.

CRITERION #2: DEFINE:

INTENT: Formulate the stakeholder problem. Define the problem, needs and objectives.

In my belief, the answer to this question is clearly defined:

5 Strongly Agree

4 Agree

3 Neutral

2 Disagree

1 Strongly Disagree

1. What customer feedback methods were used to solicit their input?
<--- Score

2. Who defines (or who defined) the rules and roles?
<--- Score

3. Has the D2L work been fairly and/or equitably divided and delegated among team members who

are qualified and capable to perform the work? Has everyone contributed?
<--- Score

4. Does the scope remain the same?
<--- Score

5. What key stakeholder process output measure(s) does D2L leverage and how?
<--- Score

6. Has a team charter been developed and communicated?
<--- Score

7. Scope of sensitive information?
<--- Score

8. What system do you use for gathering D2L information?
<--- Score

9. Is D2L required?
<--- Score

10. What would be the goal or target for a D2L's improvement team?
<--- Score

11. Is scope creep really all bad news?
<--- Score

12. What is the scope of D2L?
<--- Score

13. Is the improvement team aware of the different

versions of a process: what they think it is vs. what it actually is vs. what it should be vs. what it could be?
<--- Score

14. What are the boundaries of the scope? What is in bounds and what is not? What is the start point? What is the stop point?
<--- Score

15. Have specific policy objectives been defined?
<--- Score

16. What is the context?
<--- Score

17. What gets examined?
<--- Score

18. How do you gather D2L requirements?
<--- Score

19. What is out of scope?
<--- Score

20. What is the scope?
<--- Score

21. The political context: who holds power?
<--- Score

22. Has anyone else (internal or external to the group) attempted to solve this problem or a similar one before? If so, what knowledge can be leveraged from these previous efforts?
<--- Score

23. How do you hand over D2L context?
<--- Score

24. What are the compelling stakeholder reasons for embarking on D2L?
<--- Score

25. What are the Roles and Responsibilities for each team member and its leadership? Where is this documented?
<--- Score

26. Is D2L currently on schedule according to the plan?
<--- Score

27. How and when will the baselines be defined?
<--- Score

28. How do you think the partners involved in D2L would have defined success?
<--- Score

29. What are (control) requirements for D2L Information?
<--- Score

30. Is special D2L user knowledge required?
<--- Score

31. Are there any constraints known that bear on the ability to perform D2L work? How is the team addressing them?
<--- Score

32. Have all basic functions of D2L been defined?

<--- Score

33. What are the tasks and definitions?
<--- Score

34. Do the problem and goal statements meet the SMART criteria (specific, measurable, attainable, relevant, and time-bound)?
<--- Score

35. How do you gather requirements?
<--- Score

36. What specifically is the problem? Where does it occur? When does it occur? What is its extent?
<--- Score

37. Has everyone on the team, including the team leaders, been properly trained?
<--- Score

38. Who is gathering information?
<--- Score

39. How do you gather the stories?
<--- Score

40. What are the rough order estimates on cost savings/opportunities that D2L brings?
<--- Score

41. How do you manage unclear D2L requirements?
<--- Score

42. Are required metrics defined, what are they?
<--- Score

43. What sort of initial information to gather?
<--- Score

44. How do you build the right business case?
<--- Score

45. What is in the scope and what is not in scope?
<--- Score

46. What defines best in class?
<--- Score

47. How would you define the culture at your organization, how susceptible is it to D2L changes?
<--- Score

48. How was the 'as is' process map developed, reviewed, verified and validated?
<--- Score

49. How will the D2L team and the group measure complete success of D2L?
<--- Score

50. Is the D2L scope complete and appropriately sized?
<--- Score

51. What is the scope of the D2L work?
<--- Score

52. Is there any additional D2L definition of success?
<--- Score

53. Do you have a D2L success story or case study

ready to tell and share?
<--- Score

54. Is data collected and displayed to better understand customer(s) critical needs and requirements.
<--- Score

55. What D2L services do you require?
<--- Score

56. What knowledge or experience is required?
<--- Score

57. How is the team tracking and documenting its work?
<--- Score

58. What are the record-keeping requirements of D2L activities?
<--- Score

59. Does the team have regular meetings?
<--- Score

60. How did the D2L manager receive input to the development of a D2L improvement plan and the estimated completion dates/times of each activity?
<--- Score

61. What is in scope?
<--- Score

62. Is the D2L scope manageable?
<--- Score

63. Will a D2L production readiness review be required?
<--- Score

64. Is the work to date meeting requirements?
<--- Score

65. Is there a critical path to deliver D2L results?
<--- Score

66. Has a D2L requirement not been met?
<--- Score

67. How does the D2L manager ensure against scope creep?
<--- Score

68. Who approved the D2L scope?
<--- Score

69. Is the team adequately staffed with the desired cross-functionality? If not, what additional resources are available to the team?
<--- Score

70. Is there a completed, verified, and validated high-level 'as is' (not 'should be' or 'could be') stakeholder process map?
<--- Score

71. If substitutes have been appointed, have they been briefed on the D2L goals and received regular communications as to the progress to date?
<--- Score

72. Is there a D2L management charter, including

stakeholder case, problem and goal statements, scope, milestones, roles and responsibilities, communication plan?
<--- Score

73. Have all of the relationships been defined properly?
<--- Score

74. Are there different segments of customers?
<--- Score

75. Who is gathering D2L information?
<--- Score

76. Why are you doing D2L and what is the scope?
<--- Score

77. How do you manage scope?
<--- Score

78. What is the definition of D2L excellence?
<--- Score

79. What D2L requirements should be gathered?
<--- Score

80. Who are the D2L improvement team members, including Management Leads and Coaches?
<--- Score

81. What is the definition of success?
<--- Score

82. In what way can you redefine the criteria of choice clients have in your category in your favor?

<--- Score

83. Are audit criteria, scope, frequency and methods defined?
<--- Score

84. Is the team equipped with available and reliable resources?
<--- Score

85. What information do you gather?
<--- Score

86. Are task requirements clearly defined?
<--- Score

87. Are customer(s) identified and segmented according to their different needs and requirements?
<--- Score

88. Is there regularly 100% attendance at the team meetings? If not, have appointed substitutes attended to preserve cross-functionality and full representation?
<--- Score

89. What happens if D2L's scope changes?
<--- Score

90. Has/have the customer(s) been identified?
<--- Score

91. What critical content must be communicated – who, what, when, where, and how?
<--- Score

92. Has the improvement team collected the 'voice of the customer' (obtained feedback – qualitative and quantitative)?
<--- Score

93. Has a high-level 'as is' process map been completed, verified and validated?
<--- Score

94. What are the requirements for audit information?
<--- Score

95. Has your scope been defined?
<--- Score

96. Are resources adequate for the scope?
<--- Score

97. Is D2L linked to key stakeholder goals and objectives?
<--- Score

98. What are the D2L use cases?
<--- Score

99. Do you all define D2L in the same way?
<--- Score

100. How often are the team meetings?
<--- Score

101. When is/was the D2L start date?
<--- Score

102. Are accountability and ownership for D2L clearly defined?

<--- Score

103. When are meeting minutes sent out? Who is on the distribution list?
<--- Score

104. Has a project plan, Gantt chart, or similar been developed/completed?
<--- Score

105. Has the direction changed at all during the course of D2L? If so, when did it change and why?
<--- Score

106. Is it clearly defined in and to your organization what you do?
<--- Score

107. How do you keep key subject matter experts in the loop?
<--- Score

108. How can the value of D2L be defined?
<--- Score

109. What was the context?
<--- Score

110. Is the current 'as is' process being followed? If not, what are the discrepancies?
<--- Score

111. Have the customer needs been translated into specific, measurable requirements? How?
<--- Score

112. Are different versions of process maps needed to account for the different types of inputs?
<--- Score

113. What are the D2L tasks and definitions?
<--- Score

114. Is the scope of D2L defined?
<--- Score

115. What is a worst-case scenario for losses?
<--- Score

116. Will team members regularly document their D2L work?
<--- Score

117. What scope do you want your strategy to cover?
<--- Score

118. Are the D2L requirements complete?
<--- Score

119. Are all requirements met?
<--- Score

120. What is the worst case scenario?
<--- Score

121. Where can you gather more information?
<--- Score

122. How do you manage changes in D2L requirements?
<--- Score

123. When is the estimated completion date?
<--- Score

124. What information should you gather?
<--- Score

125. What constraints exist that might impact the team?
<--- Score

126. Do you have organizational privacy requirements?
<--- Score

127. What baselines are required to be defined and managed?
<--- Score

128. Are the D2L requirements testable?
<--- Score

129. Is there a completed SIPOC representation, describing the Suppliers, Inputs, Process, Outputs, and Customers?
<--- Score

130. How will variation in the actual durations of each activity be dealt with to ensure that the expected D2L results are met?
<--- Score

131. How do you catch D2L definition inconsistencies?
<--- Score

132. What are the dynamics of the communication plan?

<--- Score

133. What is out-of-scope initially?
<--- Score

134. What is the scope of the D2L effort?
<--- Score

135. How have you defined all D2L requirements first?
<--- Score

136. How are consistent D2L definitions important?
<--- Score

137. What scope to assess?
<--- Score

Add up total points for this section:
_____ = Total points for this section

Divided by: _____ (number of
statements answered) = _____
Average score for this section

Transfer your score to the D2L Index at
the beginning of the Self-Assessment.

CRITERION #3: MEASURE:

INTENT: Gather the correct data.
Measure the current performance and
evolution of the situation.

In my belief, the answer to this
question is clearly defined:

5 Strongly Agree

4 Agree

3 Neutral

2 Disagree

1 Strongly Disagree

1. What is the total cost related to deploying D2L,
including any consulting or professional services?
<--- Score

2. What are the D2L key cost drivers?
<--- Score

3. How do you measure efficient delivery of D2L
services?

<--- Score

4. When should you bother with diagrams?
<--- Score

5. What is the total fixed cost?
<--- Score

6. What are the types and number of measures to use?
<--- Score

7. How do you aggregate measures across priorities?
<--- Score

8. What are the estimated costs of proposed changes?
<--- Score

9. What is your decision requirements diagram?
<--- Score

10. Have you included everything in your D2L cost models?
<--- Score

11. What are the D2L investment costs?
<--- Score

12. Do the benefits outweigh the costs?
<--- Score

13. How can you reduce costs?
<--- Score

14. How do you prevent mis-estimating cost?
<--- Score

15. How do you verify the authenticity of the data and information used?
<--- Score

16. What do you measure and why?
<--- Score

17. Are there competing D2L priorities?
<--- Score

18. Are you aware of what could cause a problem?
<--- Score

19. How will you measure your D2L effectiveness?
<--- Score

20. What is the root cause(s) of the problem?
<--- Score

21. What would it cost to replace your technology?
<--- Score

22. Do you effectively measure and reward individual and team performance?
<--- Score

23. What are the strategic priorities for this year?
<--- Score

24. How do you verify if D2L is built right?
<--- Score

25. How can a D2L test verify your ideas or assumptions?
<--- Score

26. When a disaster occurs, who gets priority?
<--- Score

27. Do you have any cost D2L limitation
requirements?
<--- Score

28. What are hidden D2L quality costs?
<--- Score

29. What are the current costs of the D2L process?
<--- Score

30. Is the solution cost-effective?
<--- Score

31. What users will be impacted?
<--- Score

32. How can you measure the performance?
<--- Score

33. Which costs should be taken into account?
<--- Score

34. How will success or failure be measured?
<--- Score

35. What are allowable costs?
<--- Score

36. Is there an opportunity to verify requirements?
<--- Score

37. How will you measure success?
<--- Score

38. How will your organization measure success?
<--- Score

39. Are actual costs in line with budgeted costs?
<--- Score

40. What disadvantage does this cause for the user?
<--- Score

41. How do you verify your resources?
<--- Score

42. What could cause delays in the schedule?
<--- Score

43. How are measurements made?
<--- Score

44. Have design-to-cost goals been established?
<--- Score

45. When are costs are incurred?
<--- Score

46. What are the costs of delaying D2L action?
<--- Score

47. Are the D2L benefits worth its costs?
<--- Score

48. How to cause the change?
<--- Score

49. How can you manage cost down?
<--- Score

50. Is the cost worth the D2L effort ?
<--- Score

51. How will measures be used to manage and adapt?
<--- Score

52. What can be used to verify compliance?
<--- Score

53. Are there measurements based on task performance?
<--- Score

54. Do you aggressively reward and promote the people who have the biggest impact on creating excellent D2L services/products?
<--- Score

55. What drives O&M cost?
<--- Score

56. What would be a real cause for concern?
<--- Score

57. Are indirect costs charged to the D2L program?
<--- Score

58. What potential environmental factors impact the D2L effort?
<--- Score

59. Did you tackle the cause or the symptom?
<--- Score

60. Which D2L impacts are significant?

<--- Score

61. What are your primary costs, revenues, assets?
<--- Score

62. What tests verify requirements?
<--- Score

63. How is the value delivered by D2L being measured?
<--- Score

64. How do you measure variability?
<--- Score

65. Are the units of measure consistent?
<--- Score

66. How do you measure success?
<--- Score

67. What is an unallowable cost?
<--- Score

68. Where can you go to verify the info?
<--- Score

69. What relevant entities could be measured?
<--- Score

70. Do you have a flow diagram of what happens?
<--- Score

71. Are the measurements objective?
<--- Score

72. How sensitive must the D2L strategy be to cost?
<--- Score

73. Which measures and indicators matter?
<--- Score

74. Are missed D2L opportunities costing your organization money?
<--- Score

75. What measurements are being captured?
<--- Score

76. What causes investor action?
<--- Score

77. What are the uncertainties surrounding estimates of impact?
<--- Score

78. What methods are feasible and acceptable to estimate the impact of reforms?
<--- Score

79. How can you measure D2L in a systematic way?
<--- Score

80. Are D2L vulnerabilities categorized and prioritized?
<--- Score

81. How is progress measured?
<--- Score

82. Who pays the cost?
<--- Score

83. What details are required of the D2L cost structure?
<--- Score

84. What could cause you to change course?
<--- Score

85. What causes mismanagement?
<--- Score

86. What do people want to verify?
<--- Score

87. Is it possible to estimate the impact of unanticipated complexity such as wrong or failed assumptions, feedback, etcetera on proposed reforms?
<--- Score

88. How do you measure lifecycle phases?
<--- Score

89. Where is it measured?
<--- Score

90. What happens if cost savings do not materialize?
<--- Score

91. What is the cause of any D2L gaps?
<--- Score

92. Has a cost center been established?
<--- Score

93. Do you have an issue in getting priority?

<--- Score

94. What harm might be caused?
<--- Score

95. What does your operating model cost?
<--- Score

96. How will costs be allocated?
<--- Score

97. What evidence is there and what is measured?
<--- Score

98. Are supply costs steady or fluctuating?
<--- Score

99. Who should receive measurement reports?
<--- Score

100. What measurements are possible, practicable and meaningful?
<--- Score

101. What does a Test Case verify?
<--- Score

102. How do you verify and validate the D2L data?
<--- Score

103. How long to keep data and how to manage retention costs?
<--- Score

104. What is measured? Why?
<--- Score

105. How are costs allocated?
<--- Score

106. How do you verify the D2L requirements quality?
<--- Score

107. Was a business case (cost/benefit) developed?
<--- Score

108. What are the operational costs after D2L deployment?
<--- Score

109. Why do the measurements/indicators matter?
<--- Score

110. How do you control the overall costs of your work processes?
<--- Score

111. Will D2L have an impact on current business continuity, disaster recovery processes and/or infrastructure?
<--- Score

112. Among the D2L product and service cost to be estimated, which is considered hardest to estimate?
<--- Score

113. How do your measurements capture actionable D2L information for use in exceeding your customers expectations and securing your customers engagement?
<--- Score

114. What are your operating costs?
<--- Score

115. What is the cost of rework?
<--- Score

116. Does management have the right priorities among projects?
<--- Score

117. How frequently do you track D2L measures?
<--- Score

118. What are the costs and benefits?
<--- Score

119. What are the costs of reform?
<--- Score

120. Are you taking your company in the direction of better and revenue or cheaper and cost?
<--- Score

121. Where is the cost?
<--- Score

122. How will effects be measured?
<--- Score

123. Are there any easy-to-implement alternatives to D2L? Sometimes other solutions are available that do not require the cost implications of a full-blown project?
<--- Score

124. Have you made assumptions about the shape of

the future, particularly its impact on your customers and competitors?
<--- Score

125. How is performance measured?
<--- Score

126. What causes innovation to fail or succeed in your organization?
<--- Score

127. What causes extra work or rework?
<--- Score

128. What is the D2L business impact?
<--- Score

129. At what cost?
<--- Score

130. What are your customers expectations and measures?
<--- Score

131. What are the costs?
<--- Score

132. Are you able to realize any cost savings?
<--- Score

133. What are you verifying?
<--- Score

134. How can you reduce the costs of obtaining inputs?
<--- Score

Add up total points for this section:
_____ = Total points for this section

Divided by: _____ (number of
statements answered) = _____
Average score for this section

Transfer your score to the D2L Index at
the beginning of the Self-Assessment.

CRITERION #4: ANALYZE:

INTENT: Analyze causes, assumptions and hypotheses.

In my belief, the answer to this question is clearly defined:

5 Strongly Agree

4 Agree

3 Neutral

2 Disagree

1 Strongly Disagree

1. What D2L data do you gather or use now?
<--- Score

2. What output to create?
<--- Score

3. How do you define collaboration and team output?
<--- Score

4. How has the D2L data been gathered?

<--- Score

5. Have you defined which data is gathered how?
<--- Score

6. What process improvements will be needed?
<--- Score

7. What tools were used to narrow the list of possible causes?
<--- Score

8. How will the change process be managed?
<--- Score

9. A compounding model resolution with available relevant data can often provide insight towards a solution methodology; which D2L models, tools and techniques are necessary?
<--- Score

10. Do quality systems drive continuous improvement?
<--- Score

11. What are the D2L business drivers?
<--- Score

12. What kind of crime could a potential new hire have committed that would not only not disqualify him/her from being hired by your organization, but would actually indicate that he/she might be a particularly good fit?
<--- Score

13. Identify an operational issue in your organization,

for example, could a particular task be done more quickly or more efficiently by D2L?
<--- Score

14. Which D2L data should be retained?
<--- Score

15. Has an output goal been set?
<--- Score

16. Do staff qualifications match your project?
<--- Score

17. What will drive D2L change?
<--- Score

18. Do you, as a leader, bounce back quickly from setbacks?
<--- Score

19. What are your D2L processes?
<--- Score

20. What is the Value Stream Mapping?
<--- Score

21. Who will gather what data?
<--- Score

22. Is data and process analysis, root cause analysis and quantifying the gap/opportunity in place?
<--- Score

23. Did any value-added analysis or 'lean thinking' take place to identify some of the gaps shown on the 'as is' process map?

<--- Score

24. Where is the data coming from to measure compliance?
<--- Score

25. How do you measure the operational performance of your key work systems and processes, including productivity, cycle time, and other appropriate measures of process effectiveness, efficiency, and innovation?
<--- Score

26. How do you ensure that the D2L opportunity is realistic?
<--- Score

27. What qualifications are needed?
<--- Score

28. What quality tools were used to get through the analyze phase?
<--- Score

29. How can risk management be tied procedurally to process elements?
<--- Score

30. Are gaps between current performance and the goal performance identified?
<--- Score

31. Is there any way to speed up the process?
<--- Score

32. What tools were used to generate the list of

possible causes?
<--- Score

33. How will corresponding data be collected?
<--- Score

34. Who owns what data?
<--- Score

35. Who is involved in the management review process?
<--- Score

36. What are the personnel training and qualifications required?
<--- Score

37. Was a cause-and-effect diagram used to explore the different types of causes (or sources of variation)?
<--- Score

38. Do your leaders quickly bounce back from setbacks?
<--- Score

39. Has data output been validated?
<--- Score

40. Who is involved with workflow mapping?
<--- Score

41. What D2L data should be managed?
<--- Score

42. What conclusions were drawn from the team's data collection and analysis? How did the team reach

these conclusions?
<--- Score

43. What are your outputs?
<--- Score

44. Are all staff in core D2L subjects Highly Qualified?
<--- Score

45. Did any additional data need to be collected?
<--- Score

46. What resources go in to get the desired output?
<--- Score

47. What, related to, D2L processes does your organization outsource?
<--- Score

48. What successful thing are you doing today that may be blinding you to new growth opportunities?
<--- Score

49. Who qualifies to gain access to data?
<--- Score

50. What methods do you use to gather D2L data?
<--- Score

51. Are all team members qualified for all tasks?
<--- Score

52. Were any designed experiments used to generate additional insight into the data analysis?
<--- Score

53. How is the way you as the leader think and process information affecting your organizational culture?
<--- Score

54. Do you understand your management processes today?
<--- Score

55. Do your employees have the opportunity to do what they do best everyday?
<--- Score

56. How do you promote understanding that opportunity for improvement is not criticism of the status quo, or the people who created the status quo?
<--- Score

57. What are the necessary qualifications?
<--- Score

58. How is the D2L Value Stream Mapping managed?
<--- Score

59. Think about the functions involved in your D2L project, what processes flow from these functions?
<--- Score

60. What do you need to qualify?
<--- Score

61. What qualifications and skills do you need?
<--- Score

62. Is pre-qualification of suppliers carried out?
<--- Score

63. What were the crucial 'moments of truth' on the process map?
<--- Score

64. What did the team gain from developing a sub-process map?
<--- Score

65. How do mission and objectives affect the D2L processes of your organization?
<--- Score

66. How do you identify specific D2L investment opportunities and emerging trends?
<--- Score

67. How does the organization define, manage, and improve its D2L processes?
<--- Score

68. What are the D2L design outputs?
<--- Score

69. What types of data do your D2L indicators require?
<--- Score

70. What data do you need to collect?
<--- Score

71. What other jobs or tasks affect the performance of the steps in the D2L process?
<--- Score

72. How is D2L data gathered?
<--- Score

73. How will the D2L data be captured?
<--- Score

74. What are the revised rough estimates of the financial savings/opportunity for D2L improvements?
<--- Score

75. Who will facilitate the team and process?
<--- Score

76. What are your best practices for minimizing D2L project risk, while demonstrating incremental value and quick wins throughout the D2L project lifecycle?
<--- Score

77. Can you add value to the current D2L decision-making process (largely qualitative) by incorporating uncertainty modeling (more quantitative)?
<--- Score

78. How often will data be collected for measures?
<--- Score

79. Where can you get qualified talent today?
<--- Score

80. Is the suppliers process defined and controlled?
<--- Score

81. What process should you select for improvement?
<--- Score

82. What are your current levels and trends in key measures or indicators of D2L product and process performance that are important to and directly serve your customers? How do these results compare with

the performance of your competitors and other organizations with similar offerings?
<--- Score

83. What does the data say about the performance of the stakeholder process?
<--- Score

84. How will the data be checked for quality?
<--- Score

85. What is the D2L Driver?
<--- Score

86. What is the oversight process?
<--- Score

87. Is the required D2L data gathered?
<--- Score

88. Are you missing D2L opportunities?
<--- Score

89. When should a process be art not science?
<--- Score

90. How many input/output points does it require?
<--- Score

91. Where is D2L data gathered?
<--- Score

92. What are the disruptive D2L technologies that enable your organization to radically change your business processes?
<--- Score

93. How do you implement and manage your work processes to ensure that they meet design requirements?
<--- Score

94. How difficult is it to qualify what D2L ROI is?
<--- Score

95. What were the financial benefits resulting from any 'ground fruit or low-hanging fruit' (quick fixes)?
<--- Score

96. How do your work systems and key work processes relate to and capitalize on your core competencies?
<--- Score

97. Should you invest in industry-recognized qualifications?
<--- Score

98. What is your organizations process which leads to recognition of value generation?
<--- Score

99. What D2L data should be collected?
<--- Score

100. How is data used for program management and improvement?
<--- Score

101. Were there any improvement opportunities identified from the process analysis?
<--- Score

102. Think about some of the processes you undertake within your organization, which do you own?
<--- Score

103. Is there a strict change management process?
<--- Score

104. What is the complexity of the output produced?
<--- Score

105. What are the processes for audit reporting and management?
<--- Score

106. Are your outputs consistent?
<--- Score

107. What D2L data will be collected?
<--- Score

108. Is the gap/opportunity displayed and communicated in financial terms?
<--- Score

109. What qualifications are necessary?
<--- Score

110. What are the best opportunities for value improvement?
<--- Score

111. Have any additional benefits been identified that will result from closing all or most of the gaps?
<--- Score

112. What other organizational variables, such as reward systems or communication systems, affect the performance of this D2L process?
<--- Score

113. What are your key performance measures or indicators and in-process measures for the control and improvement of your D2L processes?
<--- Score

114. What is the cost of poor quality as supported by the team's analysis?
<--- Score

115. An organizationally feasible system request is one that considers the mission, goals and objectives of the organization, key questions are: is the D2L solution request practical and will it solve a problem or take advantage of an opportunity to achieve company goals?
<--- Score

116. What qualifies as competition?
<--- Score

117. Is the final output clearly identified?
<--- Score

118. Have the problem and goal statements been updated to reflect the additional knowledge gained from the analyze phase?
<--- Score

119. Do you have the authority to produce the output?

<--- Score

120. Are D2L changes recognized early enough to be approved through the regular process?
<--- Score

121. What is the output?
<--- Score

122. What information qualified as important?
<--- Score

123. Who gets your output?
<--- Score

124. How is the data gathered?
<--- Score

125. What are your current levels and trends in key D2L measures or indicators of product and process performance that are important to and directly serve your customers?
<--- Score

126. How do you use D2L data and information to support organizational decision making and innovation?
<--- Score

127. What systems/processes must you excel at?
<--- Score

128. What is your organizations system for selecting qualified vendors?
<--- Score

129. Is the D2L process severely broken such that a re-design is necessary?
<--- Score

130. Do several people in different organizational units assist with the D2L process?
<--- Score

131. Is the performance gap determined?
<--- Score

132. How much data can be collected in the given timeframe?
<--- Score

133. How was the detailed process map generated, verified, and validated?
<--- Score

134. Were Pareto charts (or similar) used to portray the 'heavy hitters' (or key sources of variation)?
<--- Score

135. Is there an established change management process?
<--- Score

136. Was a detailed process map created to amplify critical steps of the 'as is' stakeholder process?
<--- Score

Add up total points for this section:
_ _ _ _ _   = Total points for this section

Divided by: _ _ _ _ _ _ (number of statements answered) = _ _ _ _ _ _

Average score for this section

Transfer your score to the D2L Index at the beginning of the Self-Assessment.

CRITERION #5: IMPROVE:

INTENT: Develop a practical solution.
Innovate, establish and test the
solution and to measure the results.

In my belief, the answer to this
question is clearly defined:

5 Strongly Agree

4 Agree

3 Neutral

2 Disagree

1 Strongly Disagree

1. What went well, what should change, what can
improve?
<--- Score

2. Who makes the D2L decisions in your organization?
<--- Score

3. Who controls key decisions that will be made?
<--- Score

4. Can the solution be designed and implemented within an acceptable time period?
<--- Score

5. Explorations of the frontiers of D2L will help you build influence, improve D2L, optimize decision making, and sustain change, what is your approach?
<--- Score

6. Risk events: what are the things that could go wrong?
<--- Score

7. Who controls the risk?
<--- Score

8. Does the goal represent a desired result that can be measured?
<--- Score

9. How significant is the improvement in the eyes of the end user?
<--- Score

10. Who are the D2L decision-makers?
<--- Score

11. How are policy decisions made and where?
<--- Score

12. What resources are required for the improvement efforts?
<--- Score

13. How do you define the solutions' scope?

<--- Score

14. How do you link measurement and risk?
<--- Score

15. How will you know when its improved?
<--- Score

16. Is the D2L documentation thorough?
<--- Score

17. Would you develop a D2L Communication Strategy?
<--- Score

18. Who do you report D2L results to?
<--- Score

19. How do you improve productivity?
<--- Score

20. How can you improve performance?
<--- Score

21. How are D2L risks managed?
<--- Score

22. How do you decide how much to remunerate an employee?
<--- Score

23. What area needs the greatest improvement?
<--- Score

24. Are the key business and technology risks being managed?

<--- Score

25. What actually has to improve and by how much?
<--- Score

26. What are your current levels and trends in key measures or indicators of workforce and leader development?
<--- Score

27. How will you measure the results?
<--- Score

28. Are the risks fully understood, reasonable and manageable?
<--- Score

29. How do you measure risk?
<--- Score

30. Can you identify any significant risks or exposures to D2L third- parties (vendors, service providers, alliance partners etc) that concern you?
<--- Score

31. What lessons, if any, from a pilot were incorporated into the design of the full-scale solution?
<--- Score

32. Are risk management tasks balanced centrally and locally?
<--- Score

33. Risk factors: what are the characteristics of D2L that make it risky?
<--- Score

34. What is the D2L's sustainability risk?
<--- Score

35. Who manages D2L risk?
<--- Score

36. How do you go about comparing D2L approaches/ solutions?
<--- Score

37. Is risk periodically assessed?
<--- Score

38. How do you manage and improve your D2L work systems to deliver customer value and achieve organizational success and sustainability?
<--- Score

39. Is the D2L risk managed?
<--- Score

40. What error proofing will be done to address some of the discrepancies observed in the 'as is' process?
<--- Score

41. Do vendor agreements bring new compliance risk ?
<--- Score

42. Do you need to do a usability evaluation?
<--- Score

43. Where do the D2L decisions reside?
<--- Score

44. Have you achieved D2L improvements?
<--- Score

45. What needs improvement? Why?
<--- Score

46. Are decisions made in a timely manner?
<--- Score

47. How does your organization evaluate strategic D2L success?
<--- Score

48. Risk Identification: What are the possible risk events your organization faces in relation to D2L?
<--- Score

49. What were the underlying assumptions on the cost-benefit analysis?
<--- Score

50. Was a D2L charter developed?
<--- Score

51. At what point will vulnerability assessments be performed once D2L is put into production (e.g., ongoing Risk Management after implementation)?
<--- Score

52. What are the concrete D2L results?
<--- Score

53. How scalable is your D2L solution?
<--- Score

54. How will you know that you have improved?

<--- Score

55. Is the measure of success for D2L understandable to a variety of people?
<--- Score

56. When you map the key players in your own work and the types/domains of relationships with them, which relationships do you find easy and which challenging, and why?
<--- Score

57. Is the solution technically practical?
<--- Score

58. In the past few months, what is the smallest change you have made that has had the biggest positive result? What was it about that small change that produced the large return?
<--- Score

59. What tools were most useful during the improve phase?
<--- Score

60. What assumptions are made about the solution and approach?
<--- Score

61. For decision problems, how do you develop a decision statement?
<--- Score

62. Are procedures documented for managing D2L risks?
<--- Score

63. What tools were used to evaluate the potential solutions?
<--- Score

64. What is the team's contingency plan for potential problems occurring in implementation?
<--- Score

65. How do you improve your likelihood of success ?
<--- Score

66. What is D2L risk?
<--- Score

67. D2L risk decisions: whose call Is It?
<--- Score

68. Do you combine technical expertise with business knowledge and D2L Key topics include lifecycles, development approaches, requirements and how to make a business case?
<--- Score

69. Can you integrate quality management and risk management?
<--- Score

70. If you could go back in time five years, what decision would you make differently? What is your best guess as to what decision you're making today you might regret five years from now?
<--- Score

71. What can you do to improve?
<--- Score

72. Have you identified breakpoints and/or risk tolerances that will trigger broad consideration of a potential need for intervention or modification of strategy?
<--- Score

73. What practices helps your organization to develop its capacity to recognize patterns?
<--- Score

74. Do you cover the five essential competencies: Communication, Collaboration,Innovation, Adaptability, and Leadership that improve an organizations ability to leverage the new D2L in a volatile global economy?
<--- Score

75. How is knowledge sharing about risk management improved?
<--- Score

76. What to do with the results or outcomes of measurements?
<--- Score

77. How do you improve D2L service perception, and satisfaction?
<--- Score

78. Is the D2L solution sustainable?
<--- Score

79. Is there any other D2L solution?
<--- Score

80. How do the D2L results compare with the performance of your competitors and other organizations with similar offerings?
<--- Score

81. How will you know that a change is an improvement?
<--- Score

82. How does the team improve its work?
<--- Score

83. Are the most efficient solutions problem-specific?
<--- Score

84. What are the D2L security risks?
<--- Score

85. Do you have the optimal project management team structure?
<--- Score

86. What tools were used to tap into the creativity and encourage 'outside the box' thinking?
<--- Score

87. What is D2L's impact on utilizing the best solution(s)?
<--- Score

88. To what extent does management recognize D2L as a tool to increase the results?
<--- Score

89. Will the controls trigger any other risks?
<--- Score

90. Who will be responsible for documenting the D2L requirements in detail?
<--- Score

91. Are risk triggers captured?
<--- Score

92. Is D2L documentation maintained?
<--- Score

93. Is supporting D2L documentation required?
<--- Score

94. How risky is your organization?
<--- Score

95. What risks do you need to manage?
<--- Score

96. How can you better manage risk?
<--- Score

97. Is any D2L documentation required?
<--- Score

98. How do you measure progress and evaluate training effectiveness?
<--- Score

99. How do you deal with D2L risk?
<--- Score

100. Are events managed to resolution?
<--- Score

101. Where do you need D2L improvement?
<--- Score

102. Is the scope clearly documented?
<--- Score

103. What tools do you use once you have decided on a D2L strategy and more importantly how do you choose?
<--- Score

104. Who will be using the results of the measurement activities?
<--- Score

105. What are the implications of the one critical D2L decision 10 minutes, 10 months, and 10 years from now?
<--- Score

106. What do you want to improve?
<--- Score

107. Who are the people involved in developing and implementing D2L?
<--- Score

108. What D2L improvements can be made?
<--- Score

109. Who manages supplier risk management in your organization?
<--- Score

110. Does a good decision guarantee a good outcome?

<--- Score

111. How is continuous improvement applied to risk management?
<--- Score

112. What criteria will you use to assess your D2L risks?
<--- Score

113. Who will be responsible for making the decisions to include or exclude requested changes once D2L is underway?
<--- Score

114. Do those selected for the D2L team have a good general understanding of what D2L is all about?
<--- Score

115. What strategies for D2L improvement are successful?
<--- Score

116. Are you assessing D2L and risk?
<--- Score

117. What are the expected D2L results?
<--- Score

118. How will you recognize and celebrate results?
<--- Score

119. Who are the D2L decision makers?
<--- Score

120. How do you measure improved D2L service

perception, and satisfaction?
<--- Score

121. How do you manage D2L risk?
<--- Score

122. What is the implementation plan?
<--- Score

123. What is the risk?
<--- Score

124. What should a proof of concept or pilot accomplish?
<--- Score

125. How can you improve D2L?
<--- Score

126. For estimation problems, how do you develop an estimation statement?
<--- Score

127. How can skill-level changes improve D2L?
<--- Score

128. What improvements have been achieved?
<--- Score

129. What alternative responses are available to manage risk?
<--- Score

130. Who are the key stakeholders for the D2L evaluation?
<--- Score

131. How do you mitigate D2L risk?
<--- Score

132. What were the criteria for evaluating a D2L pilot?
<--- Score

Add up total points for this section:
_____ = Total points for this section

Divided by: _____ (number of
statements answered) = _____
Average score for this section

Transfer your score to the D2L Index at
the beginning of the Self-Assessment.

CRITERION #6: CONTROL:

In my belief, the answer to this question is clearly defined:

5 Strongly Agree

4 Agree

3 Neutral

2 Disagree

1 Strongly Disagree

1. Is there a transfer of ownership and knowledge to process owner and process team tasked with the responsibilities.
<--- Score

2. Is there documentation that will support the successful operation of the improvement?
<--- Score

3. Are suggested corrective/restorative actions indicated on the response plan for known causes to problems that might surface?
<--- Score

4. Do the viable solutions scale to future needs?
<--- Score

5. Is knowledge gained on process shared and institutionalized?
<--- Score

6. How is change control managed?
<--- Score

7. How can you best use all of your knowledge repositories to enhance learning and sharing?
<--- Score

8. How do senior leaders actions reflect a commitment to the organizations D2L values?
<--- Score

9. How do controls support value?
<--- Score

10. What should you measure to verify efficiency gains?
<--- Score

11. Who is going to spread your message?
<--- Score

12. What adjustments to the strategies are needed?
<--- Score

13. How will you measure your QA plan's effectiveness?
<--- Score

14. Who sets the D2L standards?
<--- Score

15. What are your results for key measures or indicators of the accomplishment of your D2L strategy and action plans, including building and strengthening core competencies?
<--- Score

16. Is there a control plan in place for sustaining improvements (short and long-term)?
<--- Score

17. Is new knowledge gained imbedded in the response plan?
<--- Score

18. Does the D2L performance meet the customer's requirements?
<--- Score

19. In the case of a D2L project, the criteria for the audit derive from implementation objectives, an audit of a D2L project involves assessing whether the recommendations outlined for implementation have been met, can you track that any D2L project is implemented as planned, and is it working?
<--- Score

20. How likely is the current D2L plan to come in on schedule or on budget?
<--- Score

21. Does the response plan contain a definite closed loop continual improvement scheme (e.g., plan-do-check-act)?
<--- Score

22. How widespread is its use?
<--- Score

23. How will new or emerging customer needs/requirements be checked/communicated to orient the process toward meeting the new specifications and continually reducing variation?
<--- Score

24. Does a troubleshooting guide exist or is it needed?
<--- Score

25. Does D2L appropriately measure and monitor risk?
<--- Score

26. Will existing staff require re-training, for example, to learn new business processes?
<--- Score

27. What other areas of the group might benefit from the D2L team's improvements, knowledge, and learning?
<--- Score

28. Implementation Planning: is a pilot needed to test the changes before a full roll out occurs?
<--- Score

29. How might the group capture best practices and lessons learned so as to leverage improvements?

<--- Score

30. Who controls critical resources?
<--- Score

31. Are documented procedures clear and easy to follow for the operators?
<--- Score

32. Can you adapt and adjust to changing D2L situations?
<--- Score

33. Are controls in place and consistently applied?
<--- Score

34. What should the next improvement project be that is related to D2L?
<--- Score

35. Is a response plan established and deployed?
<--- Score

36. What is the best design framework for D2L organization now that, in a post industrial-age if the top-down, command and control model is no longer relevant?
<--- Score

37. What is your plan to assess your security risks?
<--- Score

38. Who is the D2L process owner?
<--- Score

39. Can support from partners be adjusted?

<--- Score

40. Where do ideas that reach policy makers and planners as proposals for D2L strengthening and reform actually originate?
<--- Score

41. What are the known security controls?
<--- Score

42. Are the planned controls working?
<--- Score

43. Is there a documented and implemented monitoring plan?
<--- Score

44. What are the key elements of your D2L performance improvement system, including your evaluation, organizational learning, and innovation processes?
<--- Score

45. What other systems, operations, processes, and infrastructures (hiring practices, staffing, training, incentives/rewards, metrics/dashboards/scorecards, etc.) need updates, additions, changes, or deletions in order to facilitate knowledge transfer and improvements?
<--- Score

46. How will the process owner verify improvement in present and future sigma levels, process capabilities?
<--- Score

47. How do you plan for the cost of succession?

<--- Score

48. How do you monitor usage and cost?
<--- Score

49. What is the recommended frequency of auditing?
<--- Score

50. What do your reports reflect?
<--- Score

51. What D2L standards are applicable?
<--- Score

52. Is there a recommended audit plan for routine surveillance inspections of D2L's gains?
<--- Score

53. Will the team be available to assist members in planning investigations?
<--- Score

54. Is a response plan in place for when the input, process, or output measures indicate an 'out-of-control' condition?
<--- Score

55. Have new or revised work instructions resulted?
<--- Score

56. Will any special training be provided for results interpretation?
<--- Score

57. What key inputs and outputs are being measured on an ongoing basis?

<--- Score

58. Are new process steps, standards, and documentation ingrained into normal operations?
<--- Score

59. What do you stand for--and what are you against?
<--- Score

60. What are the critical parameters to watch?
<--- Score

61. Does job training on the documented procedures need to be part of the process team's education and training?
<--- Score

62. What are customers monitoring?
<--- Score

63. How will the day-to-day responsibilities for monitoring and continual improvement be transferred from the improvement team to the process owner?
<--- Score

64. What is the standard for acceptable D2L performance?
<--- Score

65. How will input, process, and output variables be checked to detect for sub-optimal conditions?
<--- Score

66. Act/Adjust: What Do you Need to Do Differently?
<--- Score

67. How will the process owner and team be able to hold the gains?

<--- Score

68. Will your goals reflect your program budget?

<--- Score

69. Do you monitor the D2L decisions made and fine tune them as they evolve?

<--- Score

70. What is your theory of human motivation, and how does your compensation plan fit with that view?

<--- Score

71. Are you measuring, monitoring and predicting D2L activities to optimize operations and profitability, and enhancing outcomes?

<--- Score

72. How will report readings be checked to effectively monitor performance?

<--- Score

73. Against what alternative is success being measured?

<--- Score

74. What do you measure to verify effectiveness gains?

<--- Score

75. How do you spread information?

<--- Score

76. You may have created your quality measures at a time when you lacked resources, technology wasn't up to the required standard, or low service levels were the industry norm. Have those circumstances changed?
<--- Score

77. What can you control?
<--- Score

78. What quality tools were useful in the control phase?
<--- Score

79. How is D2L project cost planned, managed, monitored?
<--- Score

80. Are the D2L standards challenging?
<--- Score

81. How do your controls stack up?
<--- Score

82. Is there an action plan in case of emergencies?
<--- Score

83. Who has control over resources?
<--- Score

84. Do you monitor the effectiveness of your D2L activities?
<--- Score

85. Are operating procedures consistent?
<--- Score

86. Has the improved process and its steps been standardized?
<--- Score

87. Are there documented procedures?
<--- Score

88. How do you plan on providing proper recognition and disclosure of supporting companies?
<--- Score

89. How will D2L decisions be made and monitored?
<--- Score

90. How do you select, collect, align, and integrate D2L data and information for tracking daily operations and overall organizational performance, including progress relative to strategic objectives and action plans?
<--- Score

91. How do you encourage people to take control and responsibility?
<--- Score

92. How do you establish and deploy modified action plans if circumstances require a shift in plans and rapid execution of new plans?
<--- Score

93. Is reporting being used or needed?
<--- Score

94. What is the control/monitoring plan?
<--- Score

95. Is there a standardized process?
<--- Score

96. What are you attempting to measure/monitor?
<--- Score

97. What are the performance and scale of the D2L tools?
<--- Score

98. Are there other factors to consider, as department and staff fine tune the business continuity plans?
<--- Score

Add up total points for this section:
_ _ _ _ _ = Total points for this section

Divided by: _ _ _ _ _ _ (number of statements answered) = _ _ _ _ _ _
Average score for this section

Transfer your score to the D2L Index at the beginning of the Self-Assessment.

CRITERION #7: SUSTAIN:

INTENT: Retain the benefits.

In my belief, the answer to this
question is clearly defined:

5 Strongly Agree

4 Agree

3 Neutral

2 Disagree

1 Strongly Disagree

1. If your company went out of business tomorrow,
would anyone who doesn't get a paycheck here care?
<--- Score

2. Do you have enough freaky customers in your
portfolio pushing you to the limit day in and day out?
<--- Score

3. How will you insure seamless interoperability of
D2L moving forward?
<--- Score

4. Who, on the executive team or the board, has spoken to a customer recently?
<--- Score

5. What unique value proposition (UVP) do you offer?
<--- Score

6. Why should people listen to you?
<--- Score

7. Have benefits been optimized with all key stakeholders?
<--- Score

8. What is the source of the strategies for D2L strengthening and reform?
<--- Score

9. Whom among your colleagues do you trust, and for what?
<--- Score

10. How do you engage the workforce, in addition to satisfying them?
<--- Score

11. How do you know if you are successful?
<--- Score

12. Who will provide the final approval of D2L deliverables?
<--- Score

13. Is your basic point _____ or _____?
<--- Score

14. Were lessons learned captured and communicated?
<--- Score

15. What D2L skills are most important?
<--- Score

16. What one word do you want to own in the minds of your customers, employees, and partners?
<--- Score

17. What you are going to do to affect the numbers?
<--- Score

18. Is D2L dependent on the successful delivery of a current project?
<--- Score

19. Why do and why don't your customers like your organization?
<--- Score

20. What are the top 3 things at the forefront of your D2L agendas for the next 3 years?
<--- Score

21. What is excess credit hour surcharge?
<--- Score

22. How will you know that the D2L project has been successful?
<--- Score

23. What D2L modifications can you make work for you?

<--- Score

24. How do you make it meaningful in connecting D2L with what users do day-to-day?
<--- Score

25. What are the usability implications of D2L actions?
<--- Score

26. What is a feasible sequencing of reform initiatives over time?
<--- Score

27. What are the essentials of internal D2L management?
<--- Score

28. What trophy do you want on your mantle?
<--- Score

29. What do we do when new problems arise?
<--- Score

30. What goals did you miss?
<--- Score

31. What are your personal philosophies regarding D2L and how do they influence your work?
<--- Score

32. Will there be any necessary staff changes (redundancies or new hires)?
<--- Score

33. What threat is D2L addressing?
<--- Score

34. In retrospect, of the projects that you pulled the plug on, what percent do you wish had been allowed to keep going, and what percent do you wish had ended earlier?
<--- Score

35. Do you say no to customers for no reason?
<--- Score

36. Has implementation been effective in reaching specified objectives so far?
<--- Score

37. How are you doing compared to your industry?
<--- Score

38. Are your responses positive or negative?
<--- Score

39. Are all key stakeholders present at all Structured Walkthroughs?
<--- Score

40. Where can you break convention?
<--- Score

41. What knowledge, skills and characteristics mark a good D2L project manager?
<--- Score

42. Who is responsible for D2L?
<--- Score

43. Can you break it down?
<--- Score

44. Are new benefits received and understood?
<--- Score

45. Which D2L goals are the most important?
<--- Score

46. Who will manage the integration of tools?
<--- Score

47. What may be the consequences for the performance of an organization if all stakeholders are not consulted regarding D2L?
<--- Score

48. Who are the key stakeholders?
<--- Score

49. How do you lead with D2L in mind?
<--- Score

50. What is your BATNA (best alternative to a negotiated agreement)?
<--- Score

51. What are you trying to prove to yourself, and how might it be hijacking your life and business success?
<--- Score

52. If you got fired and a new hire took your place, what would she do different?
<--- Score

53. What are the short and long-term D2L goals?
<--- Score

54. How do you keep the momentum going?
<--- Score

55. Can the schedule be done in the given time?
<--- Score

56. What are the business goals D2L is aiming to achieve?
<--- Score

57. What is the funding source for this project?
<--- Score

58. How do you ensure that implementations of D2L products are done in a way that ensures safety?
<--- Score

59. What have been your experiences in defining long range D2L goals?
<--- Score

60. Is the impact that D2L has shown?
<--- Score

61. If there were zero limitations, what would you do differently?
<--- Score

62. Who else should you help?
<--- Score

63. How can you become more high-tech but still be high touch?
<--- Score

64. If you were responsible for initiating and

implementing major changes in your organization, what steps might you take to ensure acceptance of those changes?
<--- Score

65. What must you excel at?
<--- Score

66. Do you know who is a friend or a foe?
<--- Score

67. How can you negotiate D2L successfully with a stubborn boss, an irate client, or a deceitful coworker?
<--- Score

68. Is the D2L organization completing tasks effectively and efficiently?
<--- Score

69. What are strategies for increasing support and reducing opposition?
<--- Score

70. Which models, tools and techniques are necessary?
<--- Score

71. What is the estimated value of the project?
<--- Score

72. How will you ensure you get what you expected?
<--- Score

73. Why is it important to have senior management support for a D2L project?
<--- Score

74. What would you recommend your friend do if he/she were facing this dilemma?
<--- Score

75. Who are four people whose careers you have enhanced?
<--- Score

76. What are the success criteria that will indicate that D2L objectives have been met and the benefits delivered?
<--- Score

77. How long will it take to change?
<--- Score

78. Do you think you know, or do you know you know ?
<--- Score

79. What are the long-term D2L goals?
<--- Score

80. Why is D2L important for you now?
<--- Score

81. Did your employees make progress today?
<--- Score

82. How do customers see your organization?
<--- Score

83. Who will determine interim and final deadlines?
<--- Score

84. What are specific D2L rules to follow?
<--- Score

85. What are internal and external D2L relations?
<--- Score

86. How do you provide a safe environment
-physically and emotionally?
<--- Score

87. How do you cross-sell and up-sell your D2L
success?
<--- Score

88. Do you have an implicit bias for capital
investments over people investments?
<--- Score

89. Is maximizing D2L protection the same as
minimizing D2L loss?
<--- Score

90. What are the key enablers to make this D2L move?
<--- Score

91. What could happen if you do not do it?
<--- Score

92. Who is responsible for ensuring appropriate
resources (time, people and money) are allocated to
D2L?
<--- Score

93. Which individuals, teams or departments will be
involved in D2L?
<--- Score

94. If no one would ever find out about your accomplishments, how would you lead differently?
<--- Score

95. Are you maintaining a past–present–future perspective throughout the D2L discussion?
<--- Score

96. Instead of going to current contacts for new ideas, what if you reconnected with dormant contacts--the people you used to know? If you were going reactivate a dormant tie, who would it be?
<--- Score

97. Marketing budgets are tighter, consumers are more skeptical, and social media has changed forever the way we talk about D2L, how do you gain traction?
<--- Score

98. Who do you think the world wants your organization to be?
<--- Score

99. What happens when a new employee joins the organization?
<--- Score

100. What trouble can you get into?
<--- Score

101. How do you create buy-in?
<--- Score

102. Who do you want your customers to become?
<--- Score

103. Why will customers want to buy your organizations products/services?
<--- Score

104. How do you set D2L stretch targets and how do you get people to not only participate in setting these stretch targets but also that they strive to achieve these?
<--- Score

105. If you weren't already in this business, would you enter it today? And if not, what are you going to do about it?
<--- Score

106. Which functions and people interact with the supplier and or customer?
<--- Score

107. How do you govern and fulfill your societal responsibilities?
<--- Score

108. Do you know what you are doing? And who do you call if you don't?
<--- Score

109. Is there any existing D2L governance structure?
<--- Score

110. What projects are going on in the organization today, and what resources are those projects using from the resource pools?
<--- Score

111. What should you stop doing?
<--- Score

112. What role does communication play in the success or failure of a D2L project?
<--- Score

113. Are the criteria for selecting recommendations stated?
<--- Score

114. What management system can you use to leverage the D2L experience, ideas, and concerns of the people closest to the work to be done?
<--- Score

115. Are assumptions made in D2L stated explicitly?
<--- Score

116. What is the big D2L idea?
<--- Score

117. How do senior leaders deploy your organizations vision and values through your leadership system, to the workforce, to key suppliers and partners, and to customers and other stakeholders, as appropriate?
<--- Score

118. What is the overall business strategy?
<--- Score

119. What will be the consequences to the stakeholder (financial, reputation etc) if D2L does not go ahead or fails to deliver the objectives?
<--- Score

120. Is D2L realistic, or are you setting yourself up for failure?
<--- Score

121. How much contingency will be available in the budget?
<--- Score

122. Are you paying enough attention to the partners your company depends on to succeed?
<--- Score

123. What is your question? Why?
<--- Score

124. If you had to rebuild your organization without any traditional competitive advantages (i.e., no killer technology, promising research, innovative product/ service delivery model, etcetera), how would your people have to approach their work and collaborate together in order to create the necessary conditions for success?
<--- Score

125. How do you foster innovation?
<--- Score

126. Have new benefits been realized?
<--- Score

127. What is something you believe that nearly no one agrees with you on?
<--- Score

128. What is the difference between dropping and withdrawing from a course?

<--- Score

129. Who are your customers?
<--- Score

130. What does your signature ensure?
<--- Score

131. Do you have the right capabilities and capacities?
<--- Score

132. What information is critical to your organization that your executives are ignoring?
<--- Score

133. How is implementation research currently incorporated into each of your goals?
<--- Score

134. If you had to leave your organization for a year and the only communication you could have with employees/colleagues was a single paragraph, what would you write?
<--- Score

135. Do you think D2L accomplishes the goals you expect it to accomplish?
<--- Score

136. Whose voice (department, ethnic group, women, older workers, etc) might you have missed hearing from in your company, and how might you amplify this voice to create positive momentum for your business?
<--- Score

137. If you do not follow, then how to lead?
<--- Score

138. Do you have past D2L successes?
<--- Score

139. What stupid rule would you most like to kill?
<--- Score

140. How do you stay inspired?
<--- Score

141. How do you accomplish your long range D2L goals?
<--- Score

142. What is an unauthorized commitment?
<--- Score

143. What is your formula for success in D2L ?
<--- Score

144. How does D2L integrate with other stakeholder initiatives?
<--- Score

145. Can you maintain your growth without detracting from the factors that have contributed to your success?
<--- Score

146. What would have to be true for the option on the table to be the best possible choice?
<--- Score

147. What is it like to work for you?

<--- Score

148. Do D2L rules make a reasonable demand on a users capabilities?
<--- Score

149. How will you motivate the stakeholders with the least vested interest?
<--- Score

150. How do you proactively clarify deliverables and D2L quality expectations?
<--- Score

151. How do you make it visible to employees?
<--- Score

152. Is a D2L breakthrough on the horizon?
<--- Score

153. What is your D2L strategy?
<--- Score

154. What are the barriers to increased D2L production?
<--- Score

155. Who have you, as a company, historically been when you've been at your best?
<--- Score

156. Who is responsible for errors?
<--- Score

157. To whom do you add value?
<--- Score

158. How important is D2L to the user organizations mission?
<--- Score

159. Are there any activities that you can take off your to do list?
<--- Score

160. Who will be responsible for deciding whether D2L goes ahead or not after the initial investigations?
<--- Score

161. What potential megatrends could make your business model obsolete?
<--- Score

162. Is there any reason to believe the opposite of my current belief?
<--- Score

163. Are the assumptions believable and achievable?
<--- Score

164. What is the overall talent health of your organization as a whole at senior levels, and for each organization reporting to a member of the Senior Leadership Team?
<--- Score

165. Political -is anyone trying to undermine this project?
<--- Score

166. Who do we want your customers to become?
<--- Score

167. What is the recommended frequency of auditing?
<--- Score

168. What business benefits will D2L goals deliver if achieved?
<--- Score

169. What happens if you do not have enough funding?
<--- Score

170. How can you become the company that would put you out of business?
<--- Score

171. How do you manage D2L Knowledge Management (KM)?
<--- Score

172. Will it be accepted by users?
<--- Score

173. What was the last experiment you ran?
<--- Score

174. What are the gaps in your knowledge and experience?
<--- Score

175. Operational - will it work?
<--- Score

176. Why should you adopt a D2L framework?
<--- Score

177. What did you miss in the interview for the worst hire you ever made?
<--- Score

178. What relationships among D2L trends do you perceive?
<--- Score

179. How do you determine the key elements that affect D2L workforce satisfaction, how are these elements determined for different workforce groups and segments?
<--- Score

180. What are the potential basics of D2L fraud?
<--- Score

181. How much does D2L help?
<--- Score

182. Does a D2L quantification method exist?
<--- Score

183. If you find that you havent accomplished one of the goals for one of the steps of the D2L strategy, what will you do to fix it?
<--- Score

184. What is the kind of project structure that would be appropriate for your D2L project, should it be formal and complex, or can it be less formal and relatively simple?
<--- Score

185. Do you see more potential in people than they do in themselves?

<--- Score

186. What new services of functionality will be implemented next with D2L ?
<--- Score

187. How do you track customer value, profitability or financial return, organizational success, and sustainability?
<--- Score

188. How likely is it that a customer would recommend your company to a friend or colleague?
<--- Score

189. Are you / should you be revolutionary or evolutionary?
<--- Score

190. Are you making progress, and are you making progress as D2L leaders?
<--- Score

191. Are you relevant? Will you be relevant five years from now? Ten?
<--- Score

192. What is the purpose of D2L in relation to the mission?
<--- Score

193. Are you using a design thinking approach and integrating Innovation, D2L Experience, and Brand Value?
<--- Score

194. What is your competitive advantage?
<--- Score

195. What is the range of capabilities?
<--- Score

196. Is there a work around that you can use?
<--- Score

197. What have you done to protect your business from competitive encroachment?
<--- Score

198. What are the challenges?
<--- Score

199. If your customer were your grandmother, would you tell her to buy what you're selling?
<--- Score

200. Who is the main stakeholder, with ultimate responsibility for driving D2L forward?
<--- Score

201. Think of your D2L project, what are the main functions?
<--- Score

202. Who uses your product in ways you never expected?
<--- Score

203. Are you changing as fast as the world around you?
<--- Score

204. Why not do D2L?
<--- Score

205. What counts that you are not counting?
<--- Score

206. Is a D2L team work effort in place?
<--- Score

207. Do you have the right people on the bus?
<--- Score

208. How do you keep records, of what?
<--- Score

209. In a project to restructure D2L outcomes, which stakeholders would you involve?
<--- Score

210. What is effective D2L?
<--- Score

211. Who is on the team?
<--- Score

212. Can you do all this work?
<--- Score

213. How do you go about securing D2L?
<--- Score

214. How can you incorporate support to ensure safe and effective use of D2L into the services that you provide?
<--- Score

215. How do you listen to customers to obtain actionable information?
<--- Score

216. Is it economical; do you have the time and money?
<--- Score

217. What are you challenging?
<--- Score

218. In the past year, what have you done (or could you have done) to increase the accurate perception of your company/brand as ethical and honest?
<--- Score

219. When information truly is ubiquitous, when reach and connectivity are completely global, when computing resources are infinite, and when a whole new set of impossibilities are not only possible, but happening, what will that do to your business?
<--- Score

Add up total points for this section:
_ _ _ _ _ = Total points for this section

Divided by: _ _ _ _ _ _ (number of statements answered) = _ _ _ _ _ _
Average score for this section

Transfer your score to the D2L Index at the beginning of the Self-Assessment.

D2L and Managing Projects, Criteria for Project Managers:

1.0 Initiating Process Group: D2L

1. What are the required resources?

2. Were resources available as planned?

3. What areas were overlooked on this D2L project?

4. Are the changes in your D2L project being formally requested, analyzed, and approved by the appropriate decision makers?

5. What were the challenges that you encountered during the execution of a previous D2L project that you would not want to repeat?

6. Where must it be done?

7. Will the D2L project meet the client requirements, and will it achieve the business success criteria that justified doing the D2L project in the first place?

8. What must be done?

9. The D2L project managers have maximum authority in which type of organization?

10. Specific - is the objective clear in terms of what, how, when, and where the situation will be changed?

11. What business situation is being addressed?

12. How well defined and documented were the D2L project management processes you chose to use?

13. Do you know all the stakeholders impacted by the D2L project and what needs are?

14. Do you understand the quality and control criteria that must be achieved for successful D2L project completion?

15. Did the D2L project team have the right skills?

16. Who are the D2L project stakeholders?

17. If the risk event occurs, what will you do?

18. Information sharing?

19. At which cmmi level are software processes documented, standardized, and integrated into a standard to-be practiced process for your organization?

20. Were escalated issues resolved promptly?

1.1 Project Charter: D2L

21. Who will take notes, document decisions?

22. D2L project background: what is the primary motivation for this D2L project?

23. What are some examples of a business case?

24. What goes into your D2L project Charter?

25. Assumptions and constraints: what assumptions were made in defining the D2L project?

26. What material?

27. Market – identify products market, including whether it is outside of the objective: what is the purpose of the program or D2L project?

28. When do you use a D2L project Charter?

29. Strategic fit: what is the strategic initiative identifier for this D2L project?

30. Why the improvements?

31. Who manages integration?

32. What barriers do you predict to your success?

33. How will you know that a change is an improvement?

34. Assumptions: what factors, for planning purposes, are you considering to be true?

35. Where does all this information come from?

36. What is the purpose of the D2L project?

37. When is a charter needed?

38. Why use a D2L project charter?

39. Why have you chosen the aim you have set forth?

40. Avoid costs, improve service, and/ or comply with a mandate?

1.2 Stakeholder Register: D2L

41. How will reports be created?

42. Who is managing stakeholder engagement?

43. What & Why?

44. How much influence do they have on the D2L project?

45. What is the power of the stakeholder?

46. Who are the stakeholders?

47. Who wants to talk about Security?

48. What opportunities exist to provide communications?

49. How big is the gap?

50. Is your organization ready for change?

51. What are the major D2L project milestones requiring communications or providing communications opportunities?

52. How should employers make voices heard?

1.3 Stakeholder Analysis Matrix: D2L

53. Will the impacts be local, national or international?

54. What is your Risk Management?

55. Seasonality, weather effects?

56. Cultural, attitudinal, behavioural?

57. Lack of competitive strength?

58. What tools would help you communicate?

59. What coalitions might build around the issues being tackled?

60. What makes a person a stakeholder?

61. How can you counter negative efforts?

62. Who will be affected by the D2L project?

63. Who will promote/support the D2L project, provided that they are involved?

64. Political effects?

65. What is the range you need to look at?

66. What is accountability in relation to the D2L project?

67. New technologies, services, ideas?

68. Price, value, quality?

69. How are the threatened D2L project targets being used?

70. Own known vulnerabilities?

71. Geographical, export, import?

2.0 Planning Process Group: D2L

72. What are the different approaches to building the WBS?

73. What good practices or successful experiences or transferable examples have been identified?

74. How will users learn how to use the deliverables?

75. How well defined and documented are the D2L project management processes you chose to use?

76. Do the partners have sufficient financial capacity to keep up the benefits produced by the programme?

77. How will it affect you?

78. Is the schedule for the set products being met?

79. If you are late, will anybody notice?

80. Explanation: is what the D2L project intents to solve a hard question?

81. If a task is partitionable, is this a sufficient condition to reduce the D2L project duration?

82. Professionals want to know what is expected from them; what are the deliverables?

83. What types of differentiated effects are resulting from the D2L project and to what extent?

84. What is the difference between the early schedule and late schedule?

85. Why do it D2L projects fail?

86. When developing the estimates for D2L project phases, you choose to add the individual estimates for the activities that comprise each phase. What type of estimation method are you using?

87. How well do the team follow the chosen processes?

88. Are work methodologies, financial instruments, etc. shared among departments, organizations and D2L projects?

89. Does it make any difference if you are successful?

90. Is the pace of implementing the products of the program ensuring the completeness of the results of the D2L project?

2.1 Project Management Plan: D2L

91. What data/reports/tools/etc. do program managers need?

92. What are the constraints?

93. What would you do differently?

94. Are the proposed D2L project purposes different than a previously authorized D2L project?

95. Is the appropriate plan selected based on your organizations objectives and evaluation criteria expressed in Principles and Guidelines policies?

96. What did not work so well?

97. What is the business need?

98. Are there any client staffing expectations?

99. What data/reports/tools/etc. do your PMs need?

100. Did the planning effort collaborate to develop solutions that integrate expertise, policies, programs, and D2L projects across entities?

101. Will you add a schedule and diagram?

102. When is the D2L project management plan created?

103. How can you best help your organization

to develop consistent practices in D2L project management planning stages?

104. Development trends and opportunities. What if the positive direction and vision of your organization causes expected trends to change?

105. What is risk management?

106. If the D2L project management plan is a comprehensive document that guides you in D2L project execution and control, then what should it NOT contain?

107. Are there any windfall benefits that would accrue to the D2L project sponsor or other parties?

108. Why do you manage integration?

109. Are cost risk analysis methods applied to develop contingencies for the estimated total D2L project costs?

2.2 Scope Management Plan: D2L

110. Has the budget been baselined?

111. Were D2L project team members involved in detailed estimating and scheduling?

112. Is there a formal process for updating the D2L project baseline?

113. Alignment to strategic goals & objectives?

114. Are written status reports provided on a designated frequent basis?

115. Have the procedures for identifying variances from estimates & adjusting the detailed work program been followed?

116. Has the selected plan been formulated using cost effectiveness and incremental analysis techniques?

117. Are D2L project team members involved in detailed estimating and scheduling?

118. Are changes in deliverable commitments agreed to by all affected groups & individuals?

119. Are non-critical path items updated and agreed upon with the teams?

120. Function of the configuration control board?

121. How difficult will it be to do specific activities on

this D2L project?

122. Have the key functions and capabilities been defined and assigned to each release or iteration?

123. Are the budget estimates reasonable?

124. Assess the expected stability of the scope of this D2L project how likely is it to change, how frequently, and by how much?

125. Materials available for performing the work?

126. Does the D2L project have a Quality Culture?

127. Will anyone else be involved in verifying the deliverables?

128. Are all resource assumptions documented?

129. Has a structured approach been used to break work effort into manageable components (WBS)?

2.3 Requirements Management Plan: D2L

130. Are actual resources expenditures versus planned expenditures acceptable?

131. Have stakeholders been instructed in the Change Control process?

132. Will the D2L project requirements become approved in writing?

133. What information regarding the D2L project requirements will be reported?

134. How will the information be distributed?

135. How often will the reporting occur?

136. Is requirements work dependent on any other specific D2L project or non-D2L project activities (e.g. funding, approvals, procurement)?

137. Did you provide clear and concise specifications?

138. Which hardware or software, related to, or as outcome of the D2L project is new to your organization?

139. Is stakeholder risk tolerance an important factor for the requirements process in this D2L project?

140. Business analysis scope?

141. What are you counting on?

142. How will the requirements become prioritized?

143. What went right?

144. Who is responsible for quantifying the D2L project requirements?

145. What cost metrics will be used?

146. Who is responsible for monitoring and tracking the D2L project requirements?

147. Is the system software (non-operating system) new to the IT D2L project team?

148. Do you know which stakeholders will participate in the requirements effort?

149. Do you really need to write this document at all?

2.4 Requirements Documentation: D2L

150. Can the requirement be changed without a large impact on other requirements?

151. What will be the integration problems?

152. What is the risk associated with the technology?

153. Does your organization restrict technical alternatives?

154. Basic work/business process; high-level, what is being touched?

155. How much does requirements engineering cost?

156. Can you check system requirements?

157. What if the system wasn t implemented?

158. Are there legal issues?

159. Where do you define what is a customer, what are the attributes of customer?

160. What marketing channels do you want to use: e-mail, letter or sms?

161. Who is interacting with the system?

162. Who is involved?

163. What kind of entity is a problem ?

164. Are there any requirements conflicts?

165. How can you document system requirements?

166. What is a show stopper in the requirements?

167. What are the potential disadvantages/ advantages?

168. Is the requirement properly understood?

169. How will they be documented / shared?

2.5 Requirements Traceability Matrix: D2L

170. Is there a requirements traceability process in place?

171. Describe the process for approving requirements so they can be added to the traceability matrix and D2L project work can be performed. Will the D2L project requirements become approved in writing?

172. What are the chronologies, contingencies, consequences, criteria?

173. Why use a WBS?

174. What percentage of D2L projects are producing traceability matrices between requirements and other work products?

175. How do you manage scope?

176. Why do you manage scope?

177. How small is small enough?

178. What is the WBS?

179. How will it affect the stakeholders personally in career?

180. Will you use a Requirements Traceability Matrix?

181. Do you have a clear understanding of all subcontracts in place?

2.6 Project Scope Statement: D2L

182. Are there adequate D2L project control systems?

183. Is the plan under configuration management?

184. Will the risk status be reported to management on a regular and frequent basis?

185. Is the D2L project manager qualified and experienced in D2L project management?

186. If you were to write a list of what should not be included in the scope statement, what are the things that you would recommend be described as out-of-scope?

187. Does the scope statement still need some clarity?

188. Which risks does the D2L project focus on?

189. Has the D2L project scope statement been reviewed as part of the baseline process?

190. Has everyone approved the D2L projects scope statement?

191. Will there be a Change Control Process in place?

192. Is there a Quality Assurance Plan documented and filed?

193. Will you need a statement of work?

194. Have the reports to be produced, distributed, and filed been defined?

195. Has a method and process for requirement tracking been developed?

196. Are the meetings set up to have assigned note takers that will add action/issues to the issue list?

197. What is change?

198. What is the most common tool for helping define the detail?

199. Relevant - ask yourself can you get there; why are you doing this D2L project?

200. Are there completion/verification criteria defined for each task producing an output?

2.7 Assumption and Constraint Log: D2L

201. Does the D2L project have a formal D2L project Plan?

202. Is this model reasonable?

203. Model-building: what data-analytic strategies are useful when building proportional-hazards models?

204. What if failure during recovery?

205. What weaknesses do you have?

206. What to do at recovery?

207. How many D2L project staff does this specific process affect?

208. Are there cosmetic errors that hinder readability and comprehension?

209. Is the steering committee active in D2L project oversight?

210. Does the plan conform to standards?

211. Is staff trained on the software technologies that are being used on the D2L project?

212. After observing execution of process, is it in compliance with the documented Plan?

213. What does an audit system look like?

214. Does the document/deliverable meet general requirements (for example, statement of work) for all deliverables?

215. Have adequate resources been provided by management to ensure D2L project success?

216. Have all stakeholders been identified?

217. How can you prevent/fix violations?

218. If appropriate, is the deliverable content consistent with current D2L project documents and in compliance with the Document Management Plan?

219. Does a documented D2L project organizational policy & plan (i.e. governance model) exist?

220. When can log be discarded?

2.8 Work Breakdown Structure: D2L

221. Is it still viable?

222. How big is a work-package?

223. Is it a change in scope?

224. Why is it useful?

225. When would you develop a Work Breakdown Structure?

226. Where does it take place?

227. What is the probability that the D2L project duration will exceed xx weeks?

228. What has to be done?

229. Who has to do it?

230. How much detail?

231. Can you make it?

232. Is the work breakdown structure (wbs) defined and is the scope of the D2L project clear with assigned deliverable owners?

233. When do you stop?

234. How many levels?

235. How far down?

236. When does it have to be done?

237. Why would you develop a Work Breakdown Structure?

2.9 WBS Dictionary: D2L

238. Identify potential or actual overruns and underruns?

239. What is wrong with this D2L project?

240. Evaluate the performance of operating organizations?

241. Are all affected work authorizations, budgeting, and scheduling documents amended to properly reflect the effects of authorized changes?

242. Contemplated overhead expenditure for each period based on the best information currently available?

243. Are all elements of indirect expense identified to overhead cost budgets of D2L projections?

244. Are the wbs and organizational levels for application of the D2L projected overhead costs identified?

245. Does the contractors system identify work accomplishment against the schedule plan?

246. Is work properly classified as measured effort, LOE, or apportioned effort and appropriately separated?

247. Are records maintained to show full accountability for all material purchased for the

contract, including the residual inventory?

248. Are current budgets resulting from changes to the authorized work and/or internal replanning, reconcilable to original budgets for specified reporting items?

249. Are there procedures for monitoring action items and corrective actions to the point of resolution and are corresponding procedures being followed?

250. Do work packages consist of discrete tasks which are adequately described?

251. Is cost and schedule performance measurement done in a consistent, systematic manner?

252. Changes in the current direct and D2L projected base?

253. Should you have a test for each code module?

254. The D2L projected business base for each period?

255. Are overhead cost budgets (or D2L projections) established on a facility-wide basis at least annually for the life of the contract?

256. Are detailed work packages planned as far in advance as practicable?

2.10 Schedule Management Plan: D2L

257. Have external dependencies been captured in the schedule?

258. Has a provision been made to reassess D2L project risks at various D2L project stages?

259. Is there an approved case?

260. Are there any activities or deliverables being added or gold-plated that could be dropped or scaled back without falling short of the original requirement?

261. Are meeting minutes captured and sent out after the meeting?

262. Are vendor contract reports, reviews and visits conducted periodically?

263. Does all D2L project documentation reside in a common repository for easy access?

264. What is the estimated time to complete the D2L project if status quo is maintained?

265. Do D2L project managers participating in the D2L project know the D2L projects true status first hand?

266. Has the schedule been baselined?

267. Are tasks tracked by hours?

268. What strengths do you have?

269. Are cause and effect determined for risks when they occur?

270. Who is responsible for estimating the activity durations?

271. Is there a formal set of procedures supporting Issues Management?

272. Is the critical path valid?

273. Are trade-offs between accepting the risk and mitigating the risk identified?

274. Has a quality assurance plan been developed for the D2L project?

275. Does the schedule have reasonable float?

2.11 Activity List: D2L

276. What is the probability the D2L project can be completed in xx weeks?

277. When do the individual activities need to start and finish?

278. In what sequence?

279. For other activities, how much delay can be tolerated?

280. How will it be performed?

281. What is the LF and LS for each activity?

282. Is there anything planned that does not need to be here?

283. How should ongoing costs be monitored to try to keep the D2L project within budget?

284. Can you determine the activity that must finish, before this activity can start?

285. When will the work be performed?

286. Who will perform the work?

287. How much slack is available in the D2L project?

288. Should you include sub-activities?

289. What went well?

290. What is the total time required to complete the D2L project if no delays occur?

291. What went wrong?

292. How can the D2L project be displayed graphically to better visualize the activities?

293. How detailed should a D2L project get?

294. What is your organizations history in doing similar activities?

2.12 Activity Attributes: D2L

295. Activity: what is Missing?

296. What conclusions/generalizations can you draw from this?

297. Has management defined a definite timeframe for the turnaround or D2L project window?

298. What activity do you think you should spend the most time on?

299. How many resources do you need to complete the work scope within a limit of X number of days?

300. Are the required resources available or need to be acquired?

301. How difficult will it be to complete specific activities on this D2L project?

302. Are the required resources available?

303. How else could the items be grouped?

304. Have you identified the Activity Leveling Priority code value on each activity?

305. Is there a trend during the year?

306. Which method produces the more accurate cost assignment?

307. Were there other ways you could have organized the data to achieve similar results?

308. What is missing?

309. Would you consider either of corresponding activities an outlier?

310. Do you feel very comfortable with your prediction?

311. Can more resources be added?

312. How do you manage time?

313. Resources to accomplish the work?

314. Can you re-assign any activities to another resource to resolve an over-allocation?

2.13 Milestone List: D2L

315. Do you foresee any technical risks or developmental challenges?

316. What date will the task finish?

317. Calculate how long can activity be delayed?

318. Level of the Innovation?

319. Identify critical paths (one or more) and which activities are on the critical path?

320. How late can each activity be finished and started?

321. What is the market for your technology, product or service?

322. Usps (unique selling points)?

323. It is to be a narrative text providing the crucial aspects of your D2L project proposal answering what, who, how, when and where?

324. What specific improvements did you make to the D2L project proposal since the previous time?

325. How will you get the word out to customers?

326. Sustainable financial backing?

327. Marketing - reach, distribution, awareness?

328. Legislative effects?

329. What are your competitors vulnerabilities?

330. What would happen if a delivery of material was one week late?

331. How will the milestone be verified?

2.14 Network Diagram: D2L

332. What is the completion time?

333. What activities must occur simultaneously with this activity?

334. Can you calculate the confidence level?

335. If a current contract exists, can you provide the vendor name, contract start, and contract expiration date?

336. Why must you schedule milestones, such as reviews, throughout the D2L project?

337. What activity must be completed immediately before this activity can start?

338. What job or jobs precede it?

339. Will crashing x weeks return more in benefits than it costs?

340. How confident can you be in your milestone dates and the delivery date?

341. What are the Major Administrative Issues?

342. What activities must follow this activity?

343. What is the probability of completing the D2L project in less that xx days?

344. If x is long, what would be the completion time if you break x into two parallel parts of y weeks and z weeks?

345. What controls the start and finish of a job?

346. What are the Key Success Factors?

347. Planning: who, how long, what to do?

348. What can be done concurrently?

349. What is the lowest cost to complete this D2L project in xx weeks?

2.15 Activity Resource Requirements: D2L

350. How do you handle petty cash?

351. When does monitoring begin?

352. Which logical relationship does the PDM use most often?

353. Time for overtime?

354. Why do you do that?

355. Are there unresolved issues that need to be addressed?

356. What is the Work Plan Standard?

357. Organizational Applicability?

358. What are constraints that you might find during the Human Resource Planning process?

359. Anything else?

360. How many signatures do you require on a check and does this match what is in your policy and procedures?

361. Other support in specific areas?

362. Do you use tools like decomposition and rolling-

wave planning to produce the activity list and other outputs?

2.16 Resource Breakdown Structure: D2L

363. Any changes from stakeholders?

364. Changes based on input from stakeholders?

365. What is the number one predictor of a groups productivity?

366. What is the primary purpose of the human resource plan?

367. Who delivers the information?

368. What is D2L project communication management?

369. Who will be used as a D2L project team member?

370. What can you do to improve productivity?

371. Who is allowed to see what data about which resources?

372. Who is allowed to perform which functions?

373. When do they need the information?

374. The list could probably go on, but, the thing that you would most like to know is, How long & How much?

375. What is the purpose of assigning and documenting responsibility?

376. What is the difference between % Complete and % work?

377. How should the information be delivered?

378. Goals for the D2L project. What is each stakeholders desired outcome for the D2L project?

379. Who will use the system?

2.17 Activity Duration Estimates: D2L

380. Are procedures defined for calculating cost estimates?

381. How can you use Microsoft D2L project and Excel to assist in D2L project risk management?

382. Are contingency plans created to prepare for risk events to occur?

383. Which frame seemed to be the most important and why?

384. How many different communications channels does a D2L project team with six people have?

385. Why is there a new or renewed interest in the field of D2L project management?

386. What are some crucial elements of a good D2L project plan?

387. How does poking fun at technical professionals communications skills impact the industry and educational programs?

388. Does a process exist to identify D2L project roles, responsibilities and reporting relationships?

389. Did anything besides luck make a difference between success and failure?

390. Are actual D2L project results compared with

planned or expected results to determine the variance?

391. Who has the PRIMARY responsibility to solve this problem?

392. After how many days will the lease cost be the same as the purchase cost for the equipment?

393. Are risks monitored to determine if an event has occurred or if the mitigation was successful?

394. Is the cost performance monitored to identify variances from the plan?

395. Who will be the main sponsor for it?

396. Are D2L project activities decomposed into manageable components to ensure expected management control?

397. Are activity duration estimates documented?

398. How do you enter durations, link tasks, and view critical path information?

2.18 Duration Estimating Worksheet: D2L

399. Do any colleagues have experience with your organization and/or RFPs?

400. Small or large D2L project?

401. Is the D2L project responsive to community need?

402. What is cost and D2L project cost management?

403. Define the work as completely as possible. What work will be included in the D2L project?

404. What info is needed?

405. Why estimate time and cost?

406. How should ongoing costs be monitored to try to keep the D2L project within budget?

407. What are the critical bottleneck activities?

408. When does your organization expect to be able to complete it?

409. What is the total time required to complete the D2L project if no delays occur?

410. Does the D2L project provide innovative ways for stakeholders to overcome obstacles or deliver better

outcomes?

411. Will the D2L project collaborate with the local community and leverage resources?

412. What questions do you have?

413. Is this operation cost effective?

414. What is your role?

415. What is next?

2.19 Project Schedule: D2L

416. If there are any qualifying green components to this D2L project, what portion of the total D2L project cost is green?

417. Are key risk mitigation strategies added to the D2L project schedule?

418. Is infrastructure setup part of your D2L project?

419. Your best shot for providing estimations how complex/how much work does the activity require?

420. Why do you think schedule issues often cause the most conflicts on D2L projects?

421. How detailed should a D2L project get?

422. How can you fix it?

423. Your D2L project management plan results in a D2L project schedule that is too long. If the D2L project network diagram cannot change and you have extra personnel resources, what is the BEST thing to do?

424. It allows the D2L project to be delivered on schedule. How Do you Use Schedules?

425. Why is this particularly bad?

426. Are all remaining durations correct?

427. What does that mean?

428. What is risk?

429. Meet requirements?

430. How do you know that youhave done this right?

431. Did the D2L project come in on schedule?

432. Verify that the update is accurate. Are all remaining durations correct?

433. The wbs is developed as part of a joint planning session. and how do you know that youhave done this right?

434. How do you use schedules?

2.20 Cost Management Plan: D2L

435. Schedule contingency – how will the schedule contingency be administrated?

436. Has a resource management plan been created?

437. Are enough systems & user personnel assigned to the D2L project?

438. Is the D2L project schedule available for all D2L project team members to review?

439. Is the steering committee active in D2L project oversight?

440. Weve met your goals?

441. Is there a set of procedures defining the scope, procedures, and deliverables defining quality control?

442. Are parking lot items captured?

443. Scope of work – What is the likelihood and extent of potential future changes to the D2L project scope?

444. Is an industry recognized mechanized support tool(s) being used for D2L project scheduling & tracking?

445. Change types and category – What are the types of changes and what are the techniques to report and control changes?

446. Are issues raised, assessed, actioned, and resolved in a timely and efficient manner?

447. Are post milestone D2L project reviews (PMPR) conducted with your organization at least once a year?

448. Are the appropriate IT resources adequate to meet planned commitments?

449. Personnel with expertise?

450. For cost control purposes?

451. Is there a formal process for updating the D2L project baseline?

452. Scope of work – What is the scope of work for each of the planned contracts?

453. Cost estimate preparation – What cost estimates will be prepared during the D2L project phases?

2.21 Activity Cost Estimates: D2L

454. What is the estimators estimating history?

455. Can you change your activities?

456. Who & what determines the need for contracted services?

457. Which contract type places the most risk on the seller?

458. Is costing method consistent with study goals?

459. Who determines when the contractor is paid?

460. How do you do activity recasts?

461. Is there anything unique in this D2L projects scope statement that will affect resources?

462. The impact and what actions were taken?

463. How do you treat administrative costs in the activity inventory?

464. Was the consultant knowledgeable about the program?

465. How do you manage cost?

466. What procedures are put in place regarding bidding and cost comparisons, if any?

467. Measurable - are the targets measurable?

468. Eac -estimate at completion, what is the total job expected to cost?

469. How Award?

470. What makes a good expected result statement?

471. Review – what are some common errors in activities to avoid?

472. Were decisions made in a timely manner?

473. Vac -variance at completion, how much over/ under budget do you expect to be?

2.22 Cost Estimating Worksheet: D2L

474. What will others want?

475. Ask: are others positioned to know, are others credible, and will others cooperate?

476. How will the results be shared and to whom?

477. What additional D2L project(s) could be initiated as a result of this D2L project?

478. What is the estimated labor cost today based upon this information?

479. What happens to any remaining funds not used?

480. Will the D2L project collaborate with the local community and leverage resources?

481. Who is best positioned to know and assist in identifying corresponding factors?

482. What can be included?

483. Identify the timeframe necessary to monitor progress and collect data to determine how the selected measure has changed?

484. Is the D2L project responsive to community need?

485. What is the purpose of estimating?

486. Does the D2L project provide innovative ways for stakeholders to overcome obstacles or deliver better outcomes?

487. What costs are to be estimated?

488. Can a trend be established from historical performance data on the selected measure and are the criteria for using trend analysis or forecasting methods met?

489. Is it feasible to establish a control group arrangement?

490. Value pocket identification & quantification what are value pockets?

2.23 Cost Baseline: D2L

491. Who will use corresponding metrics ?

492. Impact to environment?

493. Pcs for your new business. what would the life cycle costs be?

494. Review your risk triggers -have your risks changed?

495. Has the actual cost of the D2L project (or D2L project phase) been tallied and compared to the approved budget?

496. Have the resources used by the D2L project been reassigned to other units or D2L projects?

497. What is the reality?

498. Is there anything unique in this D2L projects scope statement that will affect resources?

499. What is it ?

500. What would the life cycle costs be?

501. How difficult will it be to do specific tasks on the D2L project?

502. Are you meeting with your team regularly?

503. Have all the product or service deliverables been

accepted by the customer?

504. How long are you willing to wait before you find out were late?

505. Have all approved changes to the cost baseline been identified and impact on the D2L project documented?

506. Is the cr within D2L project scope?

507. Does the suggested change request seem to represent a necessary enhancement to the product?

2.24 Quality Management Plan: D2L

508. What is quality and how will you ensure it?

509. Is there a Steering Committee in place?

510. How does the material compare to a regulatory threshold?

511. Have all involved stakeholders and work groups committed to the D2L project?

512. Are you meeting your customers expectations consistently?

513. Are there ways to reduce the time it takes to get something approved?

514. What worked well?

515. Why quality management?

516. When reporting to different audiences, do you vary the form or type of report?

517. What is the Quality Management Plan?

518. Where do you focus?

519. Does a prospective decision remain the same regardless of what the data show is?

520. How is staff informed of proper reporting methods?

521. How effectively was the Quality Management Plan applied during D2L project Execution?

522. What are your organizations current levels and trends for the already stated measures related to customer satisfaction/ dissatisfaction and product/ service performance?

523. What are your organizations current levels and trends for the already stated measures related to financial and marketplace performance?

524. Does the system design reflect the requirements?

525. How do you check in-coming sample material?

526. Do you keep back-up copies of any data?

2.25 Quality Metrics: D2L

527. Is there a set of procedures to capture, analyze and act on quality metrics?

528. Has risk analysis been adequately reviewed?

529. How does one achieve stability?

530. Are documents on hand to provide explanations of privacy and confidentiality?

531. What metrics do you measure?

532. Are applicable standards referenced and available?

533. What documentation is required?

534. Is material complete (and does it meet the standards)?

535. Are quality metrics defined?

536. How do you communicate results and findings to upper management?

537. Are there any open risk issues?

538. Where is quality now?

539. Filter visualizations of interest?

540. Do you know how much profit a 10% decrease in

waste would generate?

541. What happens if you get an abnormal result?

542. Which are the right metrics to use?

543. Was review conducted per standard protocols?

544. Has trace of defects been initiated?

545. What about still open problems?

546. Do you stratify metrics by product or site?

2.26 Process Improvement Plan: D2L

547. Are you making progress on the goals?

548. Has a process guide to collect the data been developed?

549. Has the time line required to move measurement results from the points of collection to databases or users been established?

550. How do you manage quality?

551. Does your process ensure quality?

552. Are you following the quality standards?

553. How do you measure?

554. What personnel are the coaches for your initiative?

555. Everyone agrees on what process improvement is, right?

556. What lessons have you learned so far?

557. Are there forms and procedures to collect and record the data?

558. Are you making progress on your improvement plan?

559. What personnel are the champions for the

initiative?

560. Are you making progress on the improvement framework?

561. The motive is determined by asking, Why do you want to achieve this goal?

562. What personnel are the sponsors for that initiative?

563. If a process improvement framework is being used, which elements will help the problems and goals listed?

2.27 Responsibility Assignment Matrix: D2L

564. Wbs elements contractually specified for reporting of status (lowest level only)?

565. What are the assumptions?

566. Changes in the direct base to which overhead costs are allocated?

567. Are control accounts opened and closed based on the start and completion of work contained therein?

568. The staff interests – is the group or the person interested in working for this D2L project?

569. Competencies and craftsmanship – what competencies are necessary and what level?

570. Does the contractor use objective results, design reviews, and tests to trace schedule?

571. With too many people labeled as doing the work, are there too many hands involved?

572. Are indirect costs charged to the appropriate indirect pools and incurring organization?

573. Budgeted cost for work performed?

574. Which resource planning tool provides

information on resource responsibility and accountability?

575. The already stated responsible for the establishment of budgets and assignment of resources for overhead performance?

576. Will too many Signing-off responsibilities delay the completion of the activity/deliverable?

577. Budgets assigned to major functional organizations?

578. How do you manage remotely to staff in other Divisions?

579. Does the contractors system include procedures for measuring the performance of critical subcontractors?

2.28 Roles and Responsibilities: D2L

580. What expectations were met?

581. Does the team have access to and ability to use data analysis tools?

582. Is the data complete?

583. What specific behaviors did you observe?

584. What is working well?

585. What is working well within your organizations performance management system?

586. Who is responsible for implementation activities and where will the functions, roles and responsibilities be defined?

587. Are your policies supportive of a culture of quality data?

588. Key conclusions and recommendations: Are conclusions and recommendations relevant and acceptable?

589. What expectations were NOT met?

590. Are D2L project team roles and responsibilities identified and documented?

591. Authority: what areas/D2L projects in your work do you have the authority to decide upon and act on

the already stated decisions?

592. What should you highlight for improvement?

593. To decide whether to use a quality measurement, ask how will you know when it is achieved?

594. What are your major roles and responsibilities in the area of performance measurement and assessment?

595. Who: who is involved?

596. Who is responsible for each task?

597. What should you do now to ensure that you are exceeding expectations and excelling in your current position?

598. Be specific; avoid generalities. Thank you and great work alone are insufficient. What exactly do you appreciate and why?

2.29 Human Resource Management Plan: D2L

599. Has a D2L project Communications Plan been developed?

600. Is the assigned D2L project manager a PMP (Certified D2L project manager) and experienced?

601. Is the structure for tracking the D2L project schedule well defined and assigned to a specific individual?

602. Are meeting objectives identified for each meeting?

603. Has your organization readiness assessment been conducted?

604. Are quality inspections and review activities listed in the D2L project schedule(s)?

605. Identify who is needed on the core D2L project team to complete D2L project deliverables and achieve its goals and objectives. What skills, knowledge and experiences are required?

606. Timeline and milestones?

607. What skills, knowledge and experiences are required?

608. Do people have the competencies to meet the

strategic objectives?

609. Have all involved D2L project stakeholders and work groups committed to the D2L project?

610. Are governance roles and responsibilities documented?

611. Have lessons learned been conducted after each D2L project release?

612. Is the D2L project schedule available for all D2L project team members to review?

613. Are there dependencies with other initiatives or D2L projects?

614. How can below standard performers be guided/developed to upgrade performance?

2.30 Communications Management Plan: D2L

615. Who to share with?

616. Are others part of the communications management plan?

617. Why manage stakeholders?

618. How did the term stakeholder originate?

619. Who is involved as you identify stakeholders?

620. How will the person responsible for executing the communication item be notified?

621. Who is the stakeholder?

622. What steps can you take for a positive relationship?

623. Do you ask; can you recommend others for you to talk with about this initiative?

624. Which stakeholders are thought leaders, influences, or early adopters?

625. How often do you engage with stakeholders?

626. What approaches to you feel are the best ones to use?

627. Who needs to know and how much?

628. What to know?

629. Who will use or be affected by the result of a D2L project?

630. Who are the members of the governing body?

631. Are the stakeholders getting the information others need, are others consulted, are concerns addressed?

632. Do you feel more overwhelmed by stakeholders?

633. Who is responsible?

2.31 Risk Management Plan: D2L

634. Are the metrics meaningful and useful?

635. How is the audit profession changing?

636. What are the cost, schedule and resource impacts of avoiding the risk?

637. Are D2L project requirements stable?

638. Why do you want risk management?

639. Do you have a mechanism for managing change?

640. What risks are tracked?

641. Monitoring -what factors can you track that will enable you to determine if the risk is becoming more or less likely?

642. Do end-users have realistic expectations?

643. How quickly does this item need to be resolved?

644. Does the customer have a solid idea of what is required?

645. Have customers been involved fully in the definition of requirements?

646. Was an original risk assessment/risk management plan completed?

647. Mitigation -how can you avoid the risk?

648. Are tools for analysis and design available?

649. Workarounds are determined during which step of risk management?

650. How quickly does each item need to be resolved?

651. How is risk identification performed?

652. How much risk can you tolerate?

653. Do benefits and chances of success outweigh potential damage if success is not attained?

2.32 Risk Register: D2L

654. Are there any knock-on effects/impact on any of the other areas?

655. Financial risk -can your organization afford to undertake the D2L project?

656. Who needs to know about this?

657. Amongst the action plans and recommendations that you have to introduce are there some that could stop or delay the overall program?

658. Budget and schedule: what are the estimated costs and schedules for performing risk-related activities?

659. Which key risks have ineffective responses or outstanding improvement actions?

660. Cost/benefit – how much will the proposed mitigations cost and how does this cost compare with the potential cost of the risk event/situation should it occur?

661. What is your current and future risk profile?

662. Manageability – have mitigations to the risk been identified?

663. Do you require further engagement?

664. Are there other alternative controls that could be

implemented?

665. How are risks graded?

666. Are implemented controls working as others should?

667. What evidence do you have to justify the likelihood score of the risk (audit, incident report, claim, complaints, inspection, internal review)?

668. What is the appropriate level of risk management for this D2L project?

669. Schedule impact/severity estimated range (workdays) assume the event happens, what is the potential impact?

670. Does the evidence highlight any areas to advance opportunities or foster good relations. If yes what steps will be taken?

671. Contingency actions - planned actions to reduce the immediate seriousness of the risk when it does occur. What should you do when?

672. What are the major risks facing the D2L project?

673. What is the reason for current performance gaps and do the risks and opportunities identified previously account for this?

2.33 Probability and Impact Assessment: D2L

674. How do risks change during a D2L project life cycle?

675. What risks are necessary to achieve success?

676. Which of your D2L projects should be selected when compared with other D2L projects?

677. Are requirements fully understood by the software engineering team and customers?

678. Are formal technical reviews part of this process?

679. Have top software and customer managers formally committed to support the D2L project?

680. Can this technology be absorbed with current level of expertise available in your organization?

681. Is the customer willing to commit significant time to the requirements gathering process?

682. Anticipated volatility of the requirements?

683. What are the channels available for distribution to the customer?

684. Do you manage the process through use of metrics?

685. Does the D2L project team have experience with the technology to be implemented?

686. Can you avoid altogether some things that might go wrong?

687. What new technologies are being explored in the same area?

688. How will economic events and trends likely affect the D2L project?

689. What will be the impact or consequence if the risk occurs?

690. Your customers business requirements have suddenly shifted because of a new regulatory statute, what now?

691. Who are the international/overseas D2L project partners (equipment supplier/supplier/consultant/contractor) for this D2L project?

692. Have you ascribed a level of confidence to every critical technical objective?

2.34 Probability and Impact Matrix: D2L

693. What is the best method for analysing the risks for different types of D2L projects?

694. Is there any sign of biased ranking?

695. How should you structure risks?

696. Are the risk data complete?

697. Sensitivity analysis -which risks will have the most impact on the D2L project?

698. Is the present organizational structure for handling the D2L project sufficient?

699. What are the current demands of the customer?

700. What will be the likely incidence of conflict with neighboring D2L projects?

701. Which of the risk factors can be avoided altogether?

702. Are flexibility and reuse paramount?

703. What will be cost of redeployment of the personnel?

704. What should be done with risks on the watch list?

705. Are compilers and code generators available and suitable for the product to be built?

706. How are you working with risks?

707. How well is the risk understood?

708. What has the D2L project manager forgotten to do?

709. Lay ground work for future returns?

710. Which should be probably done NEXT?

2.35 Risk Data Sheet: D2L

711. Potential for recurrence?

712. What are you weak at and therefore need to do better?

713. Who has a vested interest in how you perform as your organization (our stakeholders)?

714. What are the main threats to your existence?

715. Whom do you serve (customers)?

716. What if client refuses?

717. Do effective diagnostic tests exist?

718. How do you handle product safely?

719. Will revised controls lead to tolerable risk levels?

720. Has a sensitivity analysis been carried out?

721. What do people affected think about the need for, and practicality of preventive measures?

722. What is the chance that it will happen?

723. What will be the consequences if it happens?

724. What are you trying to achieve (Objectives)?

725. How can it happen?

726. What is the likelihood of it happening?

727. What are you here for (Mission)?

728. How can hazards be reduced?

2.36 Procurement Management Plan: D2L

729. Are D2L project leaders committed to this D2L project full time?

730. Are procurement deliverables arriving on time and to specification?

731. Are D2L project contact logs kept up to date?

732. Are changes in scope (deliverable commitments) agreed to by all affected groups & individuals?

733. Are cause and effect determined for risks when others occur?

734. Have D2L project team accountabilities & responsibilities been clearly defined?

735. Are internal D2L project status meetings held at reasonable intervals?

736. Is documentation created for communication with the suppliers and Vendors?

737. If standardized procurement documents are needed, where can others be found?

738. Is an industry recognized mechanized support tool(s) being used for D2L project scheduling & tracking?

739. Is stakeholder involvement adequate?

740. Was your organizations estimating methodology being used and followed?

741. What areas are overlooked on this D2L project?

742. Is it standard practice to formally commit stakeholders to the D2L project via agreements?

743. Is a stakeholder management plan in place that covers topics?

744. Is D2L project work proceeding in accordance with the original D2L project schedule?

2.37 Source Selection Criteria: D2L

745. Is experience evaluated?

746. How do you ensure an integrated assessment of proposals?

747. What is price analysis and when should it be performed?

748. How and when do you enter into D2L project Procurement Management?

749. How will you evaluate offerors proposals?

750. How are oral presentations documented?

751. Are there any common areas of weaknesses or deficiencies in the proposals in the competitive range?

752. How can business terms and conditions be improved to yield more effective price competition?

753. How should the preproposal conference be conducted?

754. How do you consolidate reviews and analysis of evaluators?

755. Are there any specific considerations that precludes offers from being selected as the awardee?

756. Who must be notified?

757. Do you have designated specific forms or worksheets?

758. What are the guidelines regarding award without considerations?

759. Does an evaluation need to include the identification of strengths and weaknesses?

760. Do you want to wait until all offerors have been evaluated?

761. Can you prevent comparison of proposals?

762. How organization are proposed quotes/prices?

763. If the costs are normalized, please account for how the normalization is conducted. Is a cost realism analysis used?

764. What should be considered when developing evaluation standards?

2.38 Stakeholder Management Plan: D2L

765. How will the equipment be verified?

766. What are reporting requirements?

767. Are D2L project leaders committed to this D2L project full time?

768. Was trending evident between audits?

769. Who might be involved in developing a charter?

770. Where to get additional help?

771. Are mitigation strategies identified?

772. Are there any potential occupational health and safety issues due to the proposed purchases?

773. Is there an issues management plan in place?

774. How are you doing/what can be done better?

775. Have you eliminated all duplicative tasks or manual efforts, where appropriate?

776. Has the scope management document been updated and distributed to help prevent scope creep?

777. Are decisions captured in a decisions log?

778. Are regulatory inspections considered part of quality control?

779. What is meant by managing the triple constraint?

780. What other teams / processes would be impacted by changes to the current process, and how?

2.39 Change Management Plan: D2L

781. What skills, education, knowledge, or work experiences should the resources have for each identified competency?

782. What are the essentials of the message?

783. Are work location changes required?

784. Who should be involved in developing a change management strategy?

785. What does a resilient organization look like?

786. Who is the target audience of the piece of information?

787. What risks may occur upfront?

788. Is there a need for new relationships to be built?

789. What new roles are needed?

790. What provokes organizational change?

791. What can you do to minimise misinterpretation and negative perceptions?

792. When does it make sense to customize?

793. What new competencies will be required for the roles?

794. What is the most positive interpretation it can receive?

795. Have the approved procedures and policies been published?

796. What type of materials/channels will be available to leverage?

797. Impact of systems implementation on organization change?

798. Who is the audience for change management activities?

799. Are there resource implications for your communications strategy?

800. How will the stakeholders share information and transfer knowledge?

3.0 Executing Process Group: D2L

801. What is the shortest possible time it will take to complete this D2L project?

802. How well did the team follow the chosen processes?

803. What are the critical steps involved in selecting measures and initiatives?

804. On which process should team members spend the most time?

805. What are crucial elements of successful D2L project plan execution?

806. Why is it important to determine activity sequencing on D2L projects?

807. If a risk event occurs, what will you do?

808. What type of people would you want on your team?

809. Have operating capacities been created and/or reinforced in partners?

810. What is the difference between using brainstorming and the Delphi technique for risk identification?

811. Does the case present a realistic scenario?

812. If action is called for, what form should it take?

813. What areas does the group agree are the biggest success on the D2L project?

814. What are deliverables of your D2L project?

815. What type of information goes in the quality assurance plan?

816. How do you measure difficulty?

817. Do your results resemble a normal distribution?

818. What are the main types of contracts if you do decide to outsource?

819. Who will provide training?

820. Is the program supported by national and/or local organizations?

3.1 Team Member Status Report: D2L

821. What is to be done?

822. Does your organization have the means (staff, money, contract, etc.) to produce or to acquire the product, good, or service?

823. Will the staff do training or is that done by a third party?

824. How does this product, good, or service meet the needs of the D2L project and your organization as a whole?

825. Does every department have to have a D2L project Manager on staff?

826. How much risk is involved?

827. What specific interest groups do you have in place?

828. Does the product, good, or service already exist within your organization?

829. Do you have an Enterprise D2L project Management Office (EPMO)?

830. How it is to be done?

831. How will resource planning be done?

832. Are the products of your organizations D2L

projects meeting customers objectives?

833. Are your organizations D2L projects more successful over time?

834. When a teams productivity and success depend on collaboration and the efficient flow of information, what generally fails them?

835. The problem with Reward & Recognition Programs is that the truly deserving people all too often get left out. How can you make it practical?

836. Why is it to be done?

837. How can you make it practical?

838. Are the attitudes of staff regarding D2L project work improving?

839. Is there evidence that staff is taking a more professional approach toward management of your organizations D2L projects?

3.2 Change Request: D2L

840. Who is communicating the change?

841. Will this change conflict with other requirements changes (e.g., lead to conflicting operational scenarios)?

842. How fast will change requests be approved?

843. Where do changes come from?

844. Who needs to approve change requests?

845. What are the duties of the change control team?

846. What are the requirements for urgent changes?

847. How do team members communicate with each other?

848. How can you ensure that changes have been made properly?

849. Are you implementing itil processes?

850. What kind of information about the change request needs to be captured?

851. Change request coordination ?

852. How is the change documented (format, content, storage)?

853. Which requirements attributes affect the risk to reliability the most?

854. What has an inspector to inspect and to check?

855. How are changes graded and who is responsible for the rating?

856. Are there requirements attributes that are strongly related to the occurrence of defects and failures?

857. What is the relationship between requirements attributes and reliability?

858. Are there requirements attributes that are strongly related to the complexity and size?

859. Has your address changed?

3.3 Change Log: D2L

860. Do the described changes impact on the integrity or security of the system?

861. Will the D2L project fail if the change request is not executed?

862. Is the submitted change a new change or a modification of a previously approved change?

863. Is the requested change request a result of changes in other D2L project(s)?

864. When was the request submitted?

865. Is this a mandatory replacement?

866. Is the change request within D2L project scope?

867. Is the change request open, closed or pending?

868. Does the suggested change request represent a desired enhancement to the products functionality?

869. Should a more thorough impact analysis be conducted?

870. Is the change backward compatible without limitations?

871. Who initiated the change request?

872. How does this relate to the standards developed

for specific business processes?

873. How does this change affect scope?

874. How does this change affect the timeline of the schedule?

875. When was the request approved?

3.4 Decision Log: D2L

876. How does an increasing emphasis on cost containment influence the strategies and tactics used?

877. How do you define success?

878. Is your opponent open to a non-traditional workflow, or will it likely challenge anything you do?

879. Is everything working as expected?

880. Do strategies and tactics aimed at less than full control reduce the costs of management or simply shift the cost burden?

881. Does anything need to be adjusted?

882. Decision-making process; how will the team make decisions?

883. Behaviors; what are guidelines that the team has identified that will assist them with getting the most out of team meetings?

884. Adversarial environment. is your opponent open to a non-traditional workflow, or will it likely challenge anything you do?

885. Who will be given a copy of this document and where will it be kept?

886. How consolidated and comprehensive a story

can you tell by capturing currently available incident data in a central location and through a log of key decisions during an incident?

887. Linked to original objective?

888. What makes you different or better than others companies selling the same thing?

889. At what point in time does loss become unacceptable?

890. What was the rationale for the decision?

891. It becomes critical to track and periodically revisit both operational effectiveness; Are you noticing all that you need to, and are you interpreting what you see effectively?

892. Who is the decisionmaker?

893. Meeting purpose; why does this team meet?

894. How does provision of information, both in terms of content and presentation, influence acceptance of alternative strategies?

895. How effective is maintaining the log at facilitating organizational learning?

3.5 Quality Audit: D2L

896. Are adequate and conveniently located toilet facilities available for use by the employees?

897. How does your organization know that its information technology system is serving its needs as effectively and constructively as is appropriate?

898. How does your organization know that its systems for assisting staff with career planning and employment placements are appropriately effective and constructive?

899. Do the suppliers use a formal quality system?

900. How does the organization know that its system for maintaining and advancing the capabilities of its staff, particularly in relation to the Mission of the organization, is appropriately effective and constructive?

901. How does your organization know that its system for attending to the health and wellbeing of its staff is appropriately effective and constructive?

902. For each device to be reconditioned, are device specifications, such as appropriate engineering drawings, component specifications and software specifications, maintained?

903. How does your organization know that its staff are presenting original work, and properly acknowledging the work of others?

904. How does your organization know that its policy management system is appropriately effective and constructive?

905. What mechanisms exist for identification of staff development needs?

906. What happens if your organization fails its Quality Audit?

907. How does your organization know that the quality of its supervisors is appropriately effective and constructive?

908. How does your organization ensure that equipment is appropriately maintained and producing valid results?

909. What does an analysis of your organizations staff profile suggest in terms of its planning, and how is this being addressed?

910. Is there a risk that information provided by management may not always be reliable?

911. How does your organization know that the range and quality of its social and recreational services and facilities are appropriately effective and constructive in meeting the needs of staff?

912. How does your organization know that its staff have appropriate access to a fair and effective grievance process?

913. What has changed/improved as a result of the

review processes?

914. Does the audit organization have experience in performing the required work for entities of your type and size?

915. Is your organizations resource allocation system properly aligned with its collection of intentions?

3.6 Team Directory: D2L

916. How and in what format should information be presented?

917. When does information need to be distributed?

918. Who will write the meeting minutes and distribute?

919. How do unidentified risks impact the outcome of the D2L project?

920. Process decisions: are all start-up, turn over and close out requirements of the contract satisfied?

921. Who will be the stakeholders on your next D2L project?

922. Days from the time the issue is identified?

923. Where should the information be distributed?

924. Do purchase specifications and configurations match requirements?

925. Process decisions: do invoice amounts match accepted work in place?

926. What needs to be communicated?

927. Is construction on schedule?

928. Process decisions: which organizational elements

and which individuals will be assigned management functions?

929. Who will report D2L project status to all stakeholders?

930. Does a D2L project team directory list all resources assigned to the D2L project?

931. Where will the product be used and/or delivered or built when appropriate?

932. Who are the Team Members?

933. When will you produce deliverables?

934. Who should receive information (all stakeholders)?

935. Decisions: is the most suitable form of contract being used?

3.7 Team Operating Agreement: D2L

936. Did you prepare participants for the next meeting?

937. Do you prevent individuals from dominating the meeting?

938. What administrative supports will be put in place to support the team and the teams supervisor?

939. Must your members collaborate successfully to complete D2L projects?

940. Do you begin with a question to engage everyone?

941. Communication protocols: how will the team communicate?

942. Did you determine the technology methods that best match the messages to be communicated?

943. Do you post meeting notes and the recording (if used) and notify participants?

944. Do you post any action items, due dates, and responsibilities on the team website?

945. What is teaming?

946. What is the anticipated procedure (recruitment, solicitation of volunteers, or assignment) for selecting team members?

947. Seconds for members to respond?

948. Do you use a parking lot for any items that are important and outside of the agenda?

949. Resource allocation: how will individual team members account for time and expenses, and how will this be allocated in the team budget?

950. Do team members reside in more than two countries?

951. What types of accommodations will be formulated and put in place for sustaining the team?

952. Are team roles clearly defined and accepted?

953. What is your unique contribution to your organization?

954. Why does your organization want to participate in teaming?

955. How will you resolve conflict efficiently and respectfully?

3.8 Team Performance Assessment: D2L

956. To what degree will the team adopt a concrete, clearly understood, and agreed-upon approach that will result in achievement of the teams goals?

957. How do you manage human resources?

958. To what degree does the team possess adequate membership to achieve its ends?

959. To what degree are the teams goals and objectives clear, simple, and measurable?

960. To what degree can team members frequently and easily communicate with one another?

961. What makes opportunities more or less obvious?

962. Individual task proficiency and team process behavior: what is important for team functioning?

963. To what degree do team members articulate the teams work approach?

964. When does the medium matter?

965. Effects of crew composition on crew performance: Does the whole equal the sum of its parts?

966. To what degree do all members feel responsible

for all agreed-upon measures?

967. To what degree are the goals ambitious?

968. To what degree do team members frequently explore the teams purpose and its implications?

969. Can team performance be reliably measured in simulator and live exercises using the same assessment tool?

970. Social categorization and intergroup behaviour: Does minimal intergroup discrimination make social identity more positive?

971. How hard did you try to make a good selection?

972. If you have criticized someones work for method variance in your role as reviewer, what was the circumstance?

973. What is method variance?

974. Does more radicalness mean more perceived benefits?

975. To what degree are the relative importance and priority of the goals clear to all team members?

3.9 Team Member Performance Assessment: D2L

976. Where can team members go for more detailed information on performance measurement and assessment?

977. How accurately is your plan implemented?

978. To what degree does the teams approach to its work allow for modification and improvement over time?

979. How is assessment information achieved, stored?

980. Are there any safeguards to prevent intentional or unintentional rating errors?

981. To what degree can the team measure progress against specific goals?

982. What evaluation results do you have?

983. Do the goals support your organizations goals?

984. What tools are available to determine whether all contract functional and compliance areas of performance objectives, measures, and incentives have been met?

985. To what degree do members articulate the goals beyond the team membership?

986. What are best practices for delivering and developing training evaluations to maximize the benefits of leveraging emerging technologies?

987. What are the staffs preferences for training on technology-based platforms?

988. Is it clear how goals will be accomplished?

989. What variables that affect team members achievement are within your control?

990. Does the rater (supervisor) have the authority or responsibility to tell an employee that the employees performance is unsatisfactory?

991. What is a significant fact or event?

992. What are best practices in use for the performance measurement system?

993. What makes them effective?

3.10 Issue Log: D2L

994. Who do you turn to if you have questions?

995. What approaches do you use?

996. Persistence; will users learn a work around or will they be bothered every time?

997. Why not more evaluators?

998. Do you prepare stakeholder engagement plans?

999. Are there potential barriers between the team and the stakeholder?

1000. What steps can you take for positive relationships?

1001. Where do team members get information?

1002. What are the stakeholders interrelationships?

1003. In your work, how much time is spent on stakeholder identification?

1004. Are you constantly rushing from meeting to meeting?

1005. What effort will a change need?

1006. Is access to the Issue Log controlled?

1007. Are stakeholder roles recognized by your

organization?

1008. In classifying stakeholders, which approach to do so are you using?

1009. What is the impact on the Business Case?

4.0 Monitoring and Controlling Process Group: D2L

1010. What were things that you need to improve?

1011. Is it what was agreed upon?

1012. What kinds of things in particular are you looking for data on?

1013. Overall, how does the program function to serve the clients?

1014. Did you implement the program as designed?

1015. How well did the chosen processes produce the expected results?

1016. Purpose: toward what end is the evaluation being conducted?

1017. How are you doing?

1018. Mitigate. what will you do to minimize the impact should a risk event occur?

1019. What areas were overlooked on this D2L project?

1020. Is the program making progress in helping to achieve the set results?

1021. Propriety: who needs to be involved in the

evaluation to be ethical?

1022. How is agile portfolio management done?

1023. Did the D2L project team have the right skills?

1024. Did it work?

1025. How well did the chosen processes fit the needs of the D2L project?

1026. How many potential communications channels exist on the D2L project?

4.1 Project Performance Report: D2L

1027. To what degree do the goals specify concrete team work products?

1028. What is the degree to which rules govern information exchange between individuals within your organization?

1029. How is the data used?

1030. To what degree can team members vigorously define the teams purpose in considerations with others who are not part of the functioning team?

1031. To what degree are the demands of the task compatible with and converge with the relationships of the informal organization?

1032. To what degree will new and supplemental skills be introduced as the need is recognized?

1033. To what degree can the team ensure that all members are individually and jointly accountable for the teams purpose, goals, approach, and work-products?

1034. To what degree does the teams purpose constitute a broader, deeper aspiration than just accomplishing short-term goals?

1035. To what degree is the team cognizant of small wins to be celebrated along the way?

1036. To what degree are the members clear on what they are individually responsible for and what they are jointly responsible for?

1037. To what degree do team members agree with the goals, relative importance, and the ways in which achievement will be measured?

1038. To what degree is there a sense that only the team can succeed?

1039. To what degree will each member have the opportunity to advance his or her professional skills in all three of the above categories while contributing to the accomplishment of the teams purpose and goals?

1040. To what degree does the task meet individual needs?

1041. To what degree are the goals realistic?

4.2 Variance Analysis: D2L

1042. When, during the last four quarters, did a primary business event occur causing a fluctuation?

1043. What is your organizations rationale for sharing expenses and services between business segments?

1044. Did your organization lose existing customers and/or gain new customers?

1045. How are material, labor, and overhead standards set?

1046. How do you verify authorization to proceed with all authorized work?

1047. What does an unfavorable overhead volume variance mean?

1048. How does your organization allocate the cost of shared expenses and services?

1049. What are the direct labor dollars and/or hours?

1050. Do you identify potential or actual budget-based and time-based schedule variances?

1051. Are there externalities from having some customers, even if they are unprofitable in the short run?

1052. Can the relationship with problem customers be restructured so that there is a win-win situation?

1053. Are significant decision points, constraints, and interfaces identified as key milestones?

1054. What are the actual costs to date?

1055. What should management do?

1056. Are indirect costs accumulated for comparison with the corresponding budgets?

1057. Are all elements of indirect expense identified to overhead cost budgets of D2L projections?

1058. Are the actual costs used for variance analysis reconcilable with data from the accounting system?

1059. Are management actions taken to reduce indirect costs when there are significant adverse variances?

1060. What types of services and expense are shared between business segments?

1061. What is the expected future profitability of each customer?

4.3 Earned Value Status: D2L

1062. How much is it going to cost by the finish?

1063. Where are your problem areas?

1064. Verification is a process of ensuring that the developed system satisfies the stakeholders agreements and specifications; Are you building the product right? What do you verify?

1065. If earned value management (EVM) is so good in determining the true status of a D2L project and D2L project its completion, why is it that hardly any one uses it in information systems related D2L projects?

1066. Earned value can be used in almost any D2L project situation and in almost any D2L project environment. it may be used on large D2L projects, medium sized D2L projects, tiny D2L projects (in cut-down form), complex and simple D2L projects and in any market sector. some people, of course, know all about earned value, they have used it for years - but perhaps not as effectively as they could have?

1067. How does this compare with other D2L projects?

1068. Validation is a process of ensuring that the developed system will actually achieve the stakeholders desired outcomes; Are you building the right product? What do you validate?

1069. Are you hitting your D2L projects targets?

1070. When is it going to finish?

1071. Where is evidence-based earned value in your organization reported?

1072. What is the unit of forecast value?

4.4 Risk Audit: D2L

1073. Are there any forms the staff is required to sign?

1074. Is there (or should there be) some impact on the process of setting materiality when the auditor more effectively identifies higher risk areas of the financial statements?

1075. What is happening in other jurisdictions? Could that happen here?

1076. Does the customer understand the process?

1077. Does your organization have any policies or procedures to guide its decision-making (code of conduct for the board, conflict of interest policy, etc.)?

1078. Management -what contingency plans do you have if the risk becomes a reality?

1079. Is safety information provided to all involved?

1080. Are the software tools integrated with each other?

1081. Do you have an understanding of insurance claims processes?

1082. Does the team have the right mix of skills?

1083. Are requirements fully understood by the team and customers?

1084. Are all financial transactions accurately recorded (receipted, banked)?

1085. What are the benefits of a Enterprise wide approach to Risk Management?

1086. For paid staff, does your organization comply with the minimum conditions for employment and/or the applicable modern award?

1087. What does your data tell you about your risks?

1088. What can be measured?

1089. Are risk assessments documented?

1090. Are enough people available?

1091. Do you promote education and training opportunities?

4.5 Contractor Status Report: D2L

1092. Describe how often regular updates are made to the proposed solution. Are corresponding regular updates included in the standard maintenance plan?

1093. What was the budget or estimated cost for your organizations services?

1094. Are there contractual transfer concerns?

1095. How long have you been using the services?

1096. If applicable; describe your standard schedule for new software version releases. Are new software version releases included in the standard maintenance plan?

1097. What was the actual budget or estimated cost for your organizations services?

1098. What was the overall budget or estimated cost?

1099. How is risk transferred?

1100. What process manages the contracts?

1101. Who can list a D2L project as organization experience, your organization or a previous employee of your organization?

1102. How does the proposed individual meet each requirement?

1103. What are the minimum and optimal bandwidth requirements for the proposed solution?

1104. What was the final actual cost?

1105. What is the average response time for answering a support call?

4.6 Formal Acceptance: D2L

1106. What was done right?

1107. How well did the team follow the methodology?

1108. Who supplies data?

1109. What features, practices, and processes proved to be strengths or weaknesses?

1110. Was the D2L project goal achieved?

1111. Does it do what D2L project team said it would?

1112. Does it do what client said it would?

1113. What lessons were learned about your D2L project management methodology?

1114. Did the D2L project manager and team act in a professional and ethical manner?

1115. What is the Acceptance Management Process?

1116. What function(s) does it fill or meet?

1117. Was the D2L project work done on time, within budget, and according to specification?

1118. Do you perform formal acceptance or burn-in tests?

1119. Did the D2L project achieve its MOV?

1120. Was business value realized?

1121. Was the client satisfied with the D2L project results?

1122. What are the requirements against which to test, Who will execute?

1123. How does your team plan to obtain formal acceptance on your D2L project?

1124. Do you buy pre-configured systems or build your own configuration?

1125. General estimate of the costs and times to complete the D2L project?

5.0 Closing Process Group: D2L

1126. How will staff learn how to use the deliverables?

1127. Were the outcomes different from the already stated planned?

1128. Contingency planning. if a risk event occurs, what will you do?

1129. Did you do things well?

1130. What areas were overlooked on this D2L project?

1131. Did the D2L project management methodology work?

1132. What will you do to minimize the impact should a risk event occur?

1133. How well did you do?

1134. Based on your D2L project communication management plan, what worked well?

1135. How well defined and documented were the D2L project management processes you chose to use?

1136. What is the amount of funding and what D2L project phases are funded?

1137. Does the close educate others to improve

performance?

1138. How well did the chosen processes fit the needs of the D2L project?

1139. What were the desired outcomes?

1140. Will the D2L project deliverable(s) replace a current asset or group of assets?

1141. What level of risk does the proposed budget represent to the D2L project?

1142. What were the actual outcomes?

5.1 Procurement Audit: D2L

1143. Are copies of policies made available to staff members involved in budget preparation and administration?

1144. What are your ethical guidelines for public procurement?

1145. Was the performance description adequate to needs and legal requirements?

1146. Did the contracting authority offer unrestricted and full electronic access to the contract documents and any supplementary documents (specifying the internet address in the notice)?

1147. Does procurement staff have recognized professional procurement qualifications or sufficient training?

1148. Is the approval graduated according to the amount disbursed?

1149. Was the estimation of contract value in accordance with the criteria fixed in the Directive?

1150. Is the routing of copies of purchase order forms defined?

1151. Does the strategy ensure that the concepts of standardisation and coordination of procurement are used to take advantage of the departments collective buying power?

1152. Were additional works strictly necessary for the completion of performance under the contract?

1153. Are all checks stored in a secure area?

1154. Are information technology resources (e-procurement) used to reduce costs?

1155. Are risks in the external environment identified, for example: Budgetary constraints?

1156. Were standards, certifications and evidence required admissible?

1157. Is there no evidence of false certifications?

1158. Are obtained prices/qualities competitive to prices/qualities obtained by other procurement functions/units, comparing obtained or improved value for money?

1159. Are regulations and protective measures in place to avoid corruption?

1160. Are the responsibilities for monitoring the execution and performance of contracts clearly assigned?

1161. What are the threats to supplier relations?

1162. Are buyers rotated so that they do not deal with the same vendors year in and year out?

5.2 Contract Close-Out: D2L

1163. Have all contracts been closed?

1164. Parties: who is involved?

1165. Have all contracts been completed?

1166. Change in knowledge?

1167. Change in circumstances?

1168. Has each contract been audited to verify acceptance and delivery?

1169. What is capture management?

1170. Why Outsource?

1171. How is the contracting office notified of the automatic contract close-out?

1172. Have all acceptance criteria been met prior to final payment to contractors?

1173. Was the contract complete without requiring numerous changes and revisions?

1174. What happens to the recipient of services?

1175. Parties: Authorized?

1176. How does it work?

1177. Was the contract type appropriate?

1178. Have all contract records been included in the D2L project archives?

1179. How/when used ?

1180. Was the contract sufficiently clear so as not to result in numerous disputes and misunderstandings?

1181. Are the signers the authorized officials?

1182. Change in attitude or behavior?

5.3 Project or Phase Close-Out: D2L

1183. What is a Risk Management Process?

1184. Who controlled key decisions that were made?

1185. Who is responsible for award close-out?

1186. What security considerations needed to be addressed during the procurement life cycle?

1187. What were the goals and objectives of the communications strategy for the D2L project?

1188. What are they?

1189. If you were the D2L project sponsor, how would you determine which D2L project team(s) and/or individuals deserve recognition?

1190. What are the informational communication needs for each stakeholder?

1191. What information did each stakeholder need to contribute to the D2L projects success?

1192. Did the delivered product meet the specified requirements and goals of the D2L project?

1193. Does the lesson educate others to improve performance?

1194. What is the information level of detail required for each stakeholder?

1195. How often did each stakeholder need an update?

1196. Have business partners been involved extensively, and what data was required for them?

1197. Planned completion date?

1198. Is there a clear cause and effect between the activity and the lesson learned?

1199. Complete yes or no?

1200. What are the marketing communication needs for each stakeholder?

5.4 Lessons Learned: D2L

1201. What worked well or did not work well, either for this D2L project or for the D2L project team?

1202. Were cost budgets met?

1203. Would you spend your own money to fix this issue?

1204. How long did redeployment take?

1205. What skills are required for the task?

1206. What would you change?

1207. What would you like to see better documented about how to use existing processes on this type of D2L project?

1208. What was the geopolitical history during the origin of your organization and at the time of task input?

1209. Did the D2L project management methodology work?

1210. How much communication is socially oriented?

1211. What is the frequency of communication?

1212. Were all interests adequately involved/ informed?

1213. How complete and timely were the materials you were provided to decide whether to proceed from one D2L project lifecycle phase to the next?

1214. How effectively and consistently was sponsorship for the D2L project conveyed?

1215. What is the supplier dependency?

1216. Who managed most of the communication within the D2L project?

1217. How well prepared were you to receive D2L project deliverables?

1218. What are the conceptual limits of the research?

1219. What things mattered the most on this D2L project?

1220. What were the main bottlenecks on the process?

Index

Assessment   6-7, 10-11, 23, 189-190, 194, 198, 206, 229-231
assets   49, 250
assign   20
assigned   137, 145, 148, 172, 187, 190, 226, 252
assigning   165
assignment   6, 156, 186-187, 227
assist   10, 71, 94, 166, 176, 220
assistant   9
assisting   222
associated   140
assume   197
Assumption   5, 146
assurance   19, 144, 153, 213
attainable   32
attained   195
attempted   30
attempting   99
attend 26
attendance   37
attended   1, 37
attending   222
attention   13, 113
attitude   254
attitudes   215
attributes   5, 140, 156, 217
audience   210-211
audiences   180
audited   253
auditing   24, 94, 118
auditor 243
audits   208
author 3
authority   69, 125, 188, 232, 251
authorized   134, 150-151, 239, 253-254
automatic   253
available   21, 35, 37, 54, 58, 86, 94, 113, 125, 137, 150, 154,
156, 172, 182, 191, 195, 198, 201, 211, 221-222, 231, 244, 251
Average   13, 27, 42, 56, 72, 87, 99, 123, 246
avoided   200
avoiding   194
awardee   206
awareness   158
background   11, 127

264

measured   18, 46, 49-52, 54-55, 74, 94, 96, 150, 230, 238, 244
measures   44, 48, 50, 54-55, 60, 65, 69-70, 76, 90, 94, 97, 181,
202, 212, 230-231, 252
measuring   96, 187
mechanical   3
mechanism   194
mechanisms   223
mechanized   172, 204
medium   229, 241
meeting   35, 39, 91, 152, 178, 180, 190, 215, 221, 223, 225,
227, 233
meetings   34, 37-38, 145, 204, 220
megatrends   117
member   7, 31, 117, 164, 214, 231, 238
members   1, 28, 36, 40, 62, 94, 136, 172, 191, 193, 212, 216,
226-233, 237-238, 251
membership   229, 231
message   89, 210
messages   227
method   119, 133, 145, 156, 174, 200, 230
methods   28, 37, 50, 62, 135, 177, 180, 227
metrics 6, 32, 93, 139, 178, 182-183, 194, 198
Microsoft   166
milestone   5, 158-160, 173
milestones   36, 129, 160, 190, 240
minimal   230
minimise   210
minimize   235, 249
minimizing   65, 109
minimum   244, 246
minority   20
minutes   39, 84, 152, 225
missed 50, 114
missing 66, 156-157
mission 64, 69, 117, 120, 203, 222
Mitigate   87, 235
mitigated   2
mitigating   153
mitigation   167, 170, 195, 208
modeling   65
models 44, 58, 107, 146
modern   244
modified   98

precede 160
precludes 206
predict127
predicting 96
prediction 157
predictor 164
pre-filled 10
prepare 166, 227, 233
prepared 1, 173, 258
present 93, 104, 110, 200, 212
presented 1, 25, 225
presenting 222
preserve 37
prevent 44, 147, 207-208, 227, 231
preventive 202
prevents 24
previous 30, 125, 158, 245
previously 134, 197, 218
prices 207, 252
primary 49, 127, 164, 167, 239
Principles 134
priorities 44-45, 54
priority 46, 51, 156, 230
privacy 41, 182
probably 164, 201
problem 17-19, 21-23, 25-28, 30, 32, 36, 45, 69, 141, 167, 215, 239, 241
problems 18-19, 21, 23, 26, 79-80, 86, 89, 103, 140, 183, 185
procedure 227
procedures 11, 79, 92, 95, 97-98, 136, 151, 153, 162, 166, 172, 174, 182, 184, 187, 211, 243
proceed 239, 258
proceeding 205
process 4, 6-9, 11, 29-30, 33, 35, 38-41, 46, 58-61, 63-71, 77, 88-89, 91-96, 98-99, 125-126, 132, 136, 138, 140, 142, 144-146, 162, 166, 173, 184-185, 198, 209, 212, 220, 223, 225, 229, 235, 241, 243, 245, 247, 249, 255, 258
processes 1, 53, 59-60, 62-64, 66-70, 91, 93, 125-126, 132-133, 209, 212, 216, 219, 224, 235-236, 243, 247, 249-250, 257
produce 1, 69, 163, 214, 226, 235
produced 68, 79, 132, 145
produces 156
producing 142, 145, 223

provokes 210
public 251
published 211
publisher 3
pulled 104
purchase 9, 167, 225, 251
purchased 150
purchases 208
purchasing 1-2
purpose 4, 11, 120, 127-128, 164-165, 176, 221, 230, 235, 237-238
purposes 128, 134, 173
pursuing 2
pushing 100
qualified 29, 62, 65, 70, 144
qualifies 62, 69
qualify 63, 67
qualifying 170
qualities 25, 252
quality 6-7, 11, 19, 46, 53, 58, 60, 66, 69, 80, 97, 116, 126, 131, 137, 144, 153, 172, 180-182, 184, 188-190, 209, 213, 222-223
quarters 239
question 12, 17, 28, 43, 57, 73, 88, 100, 113, 132, 227
questions 9-10, 12, 69, 169, 233
quickly 11, 59, 61, 194-195
quotes 207
radically 66
raised 173
ranking 200
rating 217, 231
rationale 221, 239
reached 26
reaching 104
reactivate 110
readiness 35, 190
readings 96
realism 207
realistic 26, 60, 113, 194, 212, 238
reality 178, 243
realize 2, 55
realized 113, 248
realizing 1
really 9, 25, 29, 139

social   110, 223, 230
socially 257
societal   111
software   18, 126, 138-139, 146, 198, 222, 243, 245
solicit   28
solution   1, 46, 58, 69, 73-74, 76, 78-79, 81-82, 88, 245-246
solutions   54, 74, 77, 80, 82, 89, 134
solved   23
Someone   9
someones   230
something   113, 180
Sometimes   54
Source 6, 101, 106, 206
sources   61, 71
special 31, 94
specific   10, 21, 30, 32, 39, 64, 109, 125, 136, 138, 146, 156,
158, 162, 178, 188-190, 206-207, 214, 219, 231
specified   104, 151, 186, 255
specify 237
specifying   251
spending   2
spoken 101
sponsor   25, 135, 167, 255
sponsors   20, 185
spread 89, 96
stability 137, 182
stable   194
staffed 35
staffing 20, 93, 134
staffs   232
stages   135, 152
standard   9, 95, 97, 126, 162, 183, 191, 205, 245
standards   11-12, 90, 94-95, 97, 146, 182, 184, 207, 218, 239,
252
started 10, 158
starting 11
start-up   225
stated   112, 181, 187, 189, 249
statement   5, 12, 79, 86, 144, 147, 174-175, 178
statements   13, 27, 32, 36, 42, 56, 69, 71, 87, 99, 123, 243
status   7, 63, 136, 144, 152, 186, 204, 214, 226, 241, 245
statute 199
steady 52

Made in the USA
Coppell, TX
22 July 2022

80309521R00168